# WHAT GOES AROUND COMES AROUND

*A Guide to How Life REALLY Works*

Written By

# **Rob Davis**

Property of: The RD Creative Group LLC

The RD Creative Group LLC

1 University Place, Suite 2C

New York, NY 10003

ISBN (Print Edition): 978-1-73256-650-7

ISBN (eBook Edition): 978-1-73256-651-4

*Production design by Words To Go®*

*Graphic design by Cornelius Matteo Photography*

*Editing services by Sharon Woodhouse*

*Everything Goes Media*

*Creative Group Publishing*

In Gratitude For Making Life Worthwhile

In cherished memory:

- My loving and immensely talented parents, Mildred and Humphrey, immersed till the end and together wherever.
- My wonderful sister, "The Artist," Emmie-Lee, still sculpting, painting and searching for antiques in the best thrift market in town!
- Nicholas, loving father, son, grandson and nephew.
- My best friend Billy. Twisting the night away at the Peppermint Lounge.
- Eric John, the son I never knew, but visit in his place of rest whenever possible.

So proud of:

- Sister Lenore and great hubby Frank.
- The children I've been privileged to help raise - Nan, Vanessa, Caitlin, Courtney, Genevieve and Caroline.
- The grandchildren I've been blessed to watch grow - Bryan, Joshua, Kaylie, Shai, Bodin, Aliana, Camille, Jude, and Ireland.
- Great-grandson - Wonder of Wonders - Jameson.
- Lovely great-niece - Robin.
- My friend Valbona.

Add a lifetime of great friendships, colleagues, teachers and inspiration. So much to be grateful for and I truly am.

- And to June...

# TABLE OF CONTENTS

# A Thought: *The Architect*

*We*
*are all*
*Self-made*
*But*
*Only the rich*
*Will*
*Admit it*

# ACKNOWLEDGMENTS

As is the case with all of my written and spoken commentary, I acknowledge that I borrow liberally from all my teachers including Ernest Homes, Eric Butterworth, Raymond Charles Barker, Charles and Myrtle Fillmore, Eric Pace, Stuart Grayson, Thomas Troward, Ralph Waldo Emerson, Wayne Dyer, Norman Vincent Peale, Tom Johnson, Irwin Seale, Rav Berg, Joseph Campbell and others.

In my view they would not be the least bit upset with my re-working, re-hashing, paraphrasing or any other creative interpretation of their words and the concepts they taught, so long as my intentions are pure and articulation timely.

I likewise claim no original thinking, only rather, some degree of understanding derived from years of study, living, falling, recovering, loss, gain, failure, success, pain, joy and thankfully, love.

I offer what follows in the hope that some are inspired and their life path illuminated.

# FOREWORD

I'll always remember when and where I first met Rob, in a cozy bar called The Dandelion in downtown Philadelphia. It was the meet and greet of the BookBaby Independent Authors' Conference in November 2017. Rob was there to learn about self-publishing, and sat in the only seat left in the place, which happened to be next to me! I on the other hand, was there to work, as the company where I served as Chief Operating Officer, rock paper scissors, inc, was managing the conference. It was the first such conference and my job to make sure our staff did the best possible job.

Our conversation almost immediately went to subjects like philosophy, history and alternative views of world religions. We were instant friends and could have talked for hours. I was intrigued by what he had to say about the project that had brought him to the conference, and he was refreshingly and equally, interested in my goals and views.

It was a nice first meeting, but soon ended to get back to the opening remarks of official conference. The rest of the event flew by, accompanied by a wave here and there and a few hi's in passing. It was a pleasant surprise, and now I'd even say an honor when Rob handed me a copy of his manuscript and asked if I'd read it. Getting that initial copy of this book was almost like getting to take Rob's wisdom and flair for story-telling home with me.

I've read a number of books that focus on sharing a similar message, including *"The Secret"* by Rhonda Byrne, *"The Answer"* by John Assaraf and Murray Smith, *"The Celestine Prophecy"* by James Redfield, *"Think and Grow Rich"* by Napoleon Hill, and I must say that I find Rob's to be my favorite. It's not new age gimmicky or focused on material gains. It's about taking personal responsibility for who you are and the decisions we all continuously make. I found it to be more sincere and personal, and better at explaining the important concepts it takes on, in a compelling and convincing way.

We've all read about "cause & effect" and "laws of nature." We can easily see in others and the world around us how they work. Rob's stories, examples of people he's known over the years, his own life, and current events help bring the focus to greater understanding of how it plays out in our own lives, how we build character – and from that a worthwhile life. It's about a more mindful approach to managing thoughts, words and actions.

Considering all that's happening around us in the world today, this book could not come at a better time, or be more important. As individuals and collectively, we should behave better. Rob's reasoned explanations help us to understand why. That even though fewer of us may ascribe to traditional, organized religion – or maybe because of that – we do want guidance that makes sense on the important questions. Guidance that doesn't require giving up logic and reason, and is believable.

*What Goes Around Comes Around* is an expression we've all heard many times. It is something we know to be true, even if we don't always live like we know it. This book, subtitled *"A Guide to How Life REALLY Works,"* makes sense, and is easy and meaningful to read in Rob's eloquent and flowing writing style. I can picture him talking with that glint in his eye, and even though you may not have met him, I hope you can too!

With so much information to consume each day I often find myself mainly skimming to cover as much as possible before moving on. Having had Rob's words to dwell on has been a welcome interlude I will return to many times. Anytime is the right time for this book to show up in your life, as its various lessons may hit home at any given time.

It may be staying mindful of how we nurture the important relationships in our life; or the examples, good or not so good, that we are continuously setting for others. It is a road map and cautionary yet inspiring entreaty to place high value on our lives and those of our loved ones, and then act in accordance by virtue of our more purposeful deployment of the thoughts we dwell on, the words we speak and the actions we take.

Personally, a favorite and essential part of the book is the set of reflections at the end titled, "Thoughts To Live By." Rob told me that I wasn't alone in that assessment. There are thirty of them, one for every day of the month, including such titles as:

- I Am Guided To Right Action
- I Put Legs On My Ideas
- I Create The Best Possible Me

These three-paragraph ruminations are like affirmations, but more. They're beautifully written, substantive, direct, and have a little bit of Rob's humor in them.

Rob and his book came into my life at an especially appropriate time. I was on the brink of turning fifty and at the challenging juncture of leaving an executive position at an established and successful public relations firm, working with people I respect and enjoy, to strike out on my own in a direction that was more meaningful to me.

I had once before, put time into a labor of love that was swallowed by the great recession, and definitely needed and welcomed the encouragement of seeing Rob's commitment, and understanding the effort required to create such a book as this – not to mention the reminder of my own need to stay vigilant about the future I am establishing for myself each and every day, with my own thoughts and words and actions!

Rob's life as a school teacher, turned stock broker, turned nonprofit foundation founder (www.HFC.org), singer/songwriter (www.rob-davis.com), athlete, friend, parent, grandfather & great-grandfather, and now author, inspires to lead wholesome and multi-dimensional lives. I've learned a lot from them, book and person these past few months, and I hope you'll allow *What Goes Around Comes Around* to serve as a guide to you as well.

Sheryl Woodhouse
*Founder, LivelihoodMatters*

# INTRODUCTION

This book is a treatise on *how life really works,* that combines important concepts with vignettes about people I have known personally, who provide relevant examples. The saying *"what goes around comes around,"* also the title of this book, is a common expression of our time for what has been described in countless iterations over the ages.

The notion is a fundamental principle of life that applies to every human being. Moreover, it is something that every person has heard in one form or another, generally understands, and would likely more or less agree on. What's more it is something we readily invoke in observations about others, and is as simple and fundamental as rain falling and flowers growing. The puzzlement has always been that while it is so easy to see, and comment on about the folly of others, it is so very hard to observe, admit to and adjust for in our own behavior and lives.

When I was a kid in elementary school, and the family went to a traditional Christian based church, it was embodied in the saying often invoked, *"As you sow, so shall you reap."* I had no idea what that meant until sometime later when I learned the *sow* part meant *to plant a seed,* including how much care and attention was taken in the process or not – and had nothing to do with needles and thread. Also that *reap* described what kind of harvest would result.

Still later, I remember the first time I heard what has become the modern version, and the title of this book. It happened when someone you'll soon meet in these pages was, in his wisest possible voice, opining on why a mutual acquaintance had suffered a debilitating comeuppance. "It's obvious," he said. *What goes around comes around!*

I was struck when I heard those words, and determined that I should think about them. I was to learn that it took a lot more than mere thinking. You'll better understand the full poignancy involved when you get to read, "*A Story About Peter.*"

It was while in the throes of trying to overcome some tragedy of my own that I attended a lecture about *The Law of Cause and Effect* and began to realize what the title really meant. I learned how I had drawn that crisis to myself by means of my own thoughts, words and actions, and that the only place to look for the reason for my subsequent dilemma was in the mirror.

Like most people, I could clearly see in others what was so hard to see in myself. It was easy for me to comment on how someone else's behavior had created obvious to expect consequences that person didn't see coming, only to go forth in my own life and create some equally foolish story.

So the truth is, there is nothing new or revolutionary about the subject being addressed in this book. Rather it is as old as old is! But it is also as important as any principle of life that exists, to get a grip on and actually be successful expressing in real life.

While a time tested truth, I intend this missive to be both unique and impactful in how the subject is addressed. First off, it comes from my voice, different from anyone heretofore who has ever attempted to clarify a universal principle of life. In fact, there has never been a person who has ever lived, who possessed the equivalent of my perspective, experience, achievements and failures, making this effort to do so as valid and more timely than any prior attempts. I say that with no reservation as I have studied so many of them.

Then, there is the format itself. We instinctively know that the most effective way to convey a message is through the power of storytelling, a device well-employed in *What Goes Around Comes Around,* which switches back and forth between principles discussed and the examples of people I have known who are perfect illustrations.

# STATEMENT OF PURPOSE

This book is written for anyone who has an interest in *how life really works,* and how to improve through that understanding, the circumstances and conditions of their life. Ideally, it will provide the knowledge needed, to build the motivation required, to change and grow.

For the honest truth is that for anyone to change their normal, well-practiced ways of doing things, they must understand the value of making the effort! They must, because the effort, the staying power required, is substantial. Otherwise, no matter how much reading the books, listening to the tapes, attending the seminars or retreats or church a person may do, when they return to life they will most likely react to people and circumstances in the same manner they always have, subsequently continuing to produce the very conditions they long to change.

That's the way it is for most humans, but not the way it has to be for you. After all, the greatest of all human traits is the freedom of choice, the ultimate right and ability to be the chooser, no matter what the circumstances, of one's own attitude, the selector of one's own way.

It can also be argued persuasively, however, that there are extenuating circumstances that may cast doubt on how *free* certain choices truly are, including place, circumstances and family of birth, religion, mental stability and other factors. Still there are inspiring tales of people who have transcended the most dire of circumstances and conditions to live full and meaningful lives that propel humankind forward.

Where this treatise comes down on the matter is that regardless of all those factors, at the end of the day, we make the decisions, we speak the words, we take the actions that plant the seeds in our own individual gardens of life. Moreover, sooner or later (more about this coming up), they will blossom – will they be beautiful tulips and roses or strangulating weeds? Our choices write the script.

It basically comes down to one of former GE Chairman, Jack Welch's favorite sayings –

*Either you control your own destiny, or someone else will!*

I hope that this will assist you in the quest of more effectively controlling yours.

# A Story About Nick

*He is at once the most ridiculous person I've known, and the most serious. Without question, however, he is clearly one of the most fun and also a great tennis buddy. Throughout his life, he retained the same quality of adventurousness and good humor that were apparent when I met him those many years ago.*

*Over that time we got to know each other well, the way you get to know someone who lives through very stressful times with you and still comes out a friend. We worked together and played together, shared triumphs and defeats. We debated life's important issues, were brutally critical of each other, shared our innermost fears, supported each other through difficult periods and had much fun together.*

*At the end of the day, Nick is way up there on a very short list of people I genuinely trust. In fact, I would even go so far as to say that Nick is one of a small handful of people who I have no doubt is actually for me, meaning he gets no pleasure from my defeats. He's on my side. He's not looking to pick me off in some way. If I was there to be taken advantage of, he wouldn't do it. Rather, he'd smack me in the head and point out my folly. "Wake up!" he might say. "Has your brain turned to mush?" I have asked myself how this came to be the case. How did this individual come to be someone who I trust?*

*In considering this question, there is one particular story that comes to mind. It was a beautiful summer day, and we'd just successfully completed a brutally difficult deal. We decided that it was totally appropriate to play hooky that afternoon and headed for a near-by tennis club to release some energy, celebrate, and have it out.*

*As usual, we went at it tooth and nail, battling over each point as if it were the last. Nick had me on the ropes at the end of the first set, when as luck would have it, I hit four seeing-eye shots in a row to pull back to even. It was set point and one which I'll never forget. Once again, Nick had me on the defensive. He'd hit a great approach shot to my backhand and come to the net for the put-away. It was normally a lethal combination, considering my anemic backhand. This time however, by some grace, I lofted a high and deep lob that he couldn't reach. Back he raced to try and get the ball on the bounce. I thought for sure that it was long. His body was between me and the ball so I couldn't see if it landed in or out. He did not hesitate, though, and immediately signaled the "in" sign. With that call, I had won the first set.*

*Now, if there was ever a time that a person would be tempted to make a bad call and cheat, that was it. If Nick had called the ball out, I couldn't have argued otherwise, since I couldn't really see where it bounced. The game score would have been back to deuce, and he would still be alive to win the set. Instead, he glared at me and said, "Damn you, Davis. How could you hit such a great shot at a time like that? Now you've really got me mad!"*

*That shot was one of many close calls over many years of games with Nick, which taught me a significant fact about his character. Namely, that Nick would rather lose than win by duplicitous means. Moreover, as anyone who has competed in sports knows, a cheat is a cheat is a cheat. There is no question in my mind that the person who would have called that shot out in order to gain unfair and unsportsmanlike advantage, would exhibit the same quality of behavior in other areas of life. However, while that one shot does not guarantee Nick's stellar behavior in all other circumstances, it actually does, from my experience of Nick in multiple situations, serve as the perfect metaphor. What's more, it is the cumulative effect of all of those observations that have formed the foundation of my genuine trust of Nick. It also serves me as a model of how steadfast I must be if I hope to instill that same trust in the people in my life.*

*Actually, that match turned into a memorable one indeed. Nick won the second set. We had just started the third when dark clouds filled the sky and large drops of rain began to fall. The courts around us emptied quickly as people scurried inside to beat the impending cloud burst. Nick was serving and yelled across the net to me.*

*"Hey Davis. You know I'm going to win this set anyway. You probably want to concede now so your wimp-ass self doesn't melt, right?"*

*"Serve you big lug," I yelled back.*

*Serve he did, and damned if we didn't finish that set in spite of the torrential downpour that ensued. There we were, two lunatics, whooping and laughing, slipping and sloshing, and battling for every point. I don't remember who won that set. Makes no difference. It was so much fun that I'll never forget it. I'll also never forget that point that Nick called in my favor to end the first set. That was Nick, and that brings us to that story about Peter.*

# A Story About Peter

*I can remember almost exactly when and where I first heard the expression. It was many moons ago and I'd just started working for a large Wall Street investment banking company. There had been a scandal of some sort and the newspapers were filled with stories about the downfall of some official who had previously been thought of as a respected and accomplished individual.*

*One of the senior members of the department I was working in, call him Peter G., was reading the articles with relish, chuckling out loud as he took in the details. As he concluded the article, he folded the paper with much fanfare and announced for anyone who cared to listen that, "the son-of-a-#!@a ? deserved exactly what he got."*

*"After all," he said wisely, "what goes around comes around." This was apparently one of his pet sayings. I'd never heard the expression before, but I tucked it away in the back of my mind. It wasn't long before I heard it again, but this time from a different source.*

*Now this fellow, Peter, was considered to be an important producer of business for the firm. He'd worked there for some time and at one point had been the sales manager, which was no longer the case. The current sales manager, had in fact, been hired by him as a salesman. The firm's top management had decided at one point that Peter was not cut out for a management position, however, and demoted him back to a strictly sales position, promoting the other fellow. This was explained as being due to Peter's, "lack of people skills, " a condition I was to witness at close hand.*

*In my new position at this firm, I happened to sit quite close to Peter and it wasn't long before I began to witness a series of incidents during which he would lose his composure. These incidents were characterized by Peter screaming at someone, face contorted in rage, veins bulging and abusive language streaming forth. The object of his onslaught always seemed to be* either his secretary or someone else he considered to be an underling that he could take out his rage on. That person was often reduced to tears and always to humiliation. These incidents were particularly notable, aside from their ferocity, due to the insignificance of their cause, which was usually something quite trivial.

These outbursts appeared to be tolerated by management because of Peter's effectiveness with clients, to whom of course, he never displayed such behavior. He was also very charming and funny in his banter with associates and generally liked by his peers, despite their cringes when he'd go off on a tirade.

There was one particularly large deal that Peter had been working on for some time. He said it was the biggest of his career and suggested that it was also the Firm's largest ever. He revealed to certain associates that its successful completion would finally bring him the recognition he so deserved. He had been sorely wounded by his demotion, even though he was fond of telling anyone who would listen that, "He hadn't enjoyed being everyone's nursemaid and psychoanalyst anyway." The Firm, he believed, would now be forced to reward him both monetarily and by promoting him to a more senior position, perhaps even a "partnership ". This deal would surely convince them that he was an indispensable and most valued asset.

The day finally arrived for the meeting between the clients and senior management of the firm, when Peter would make his formal presentation to wrap up the deal. The time was set for 3:00 P.M. Peter had already pre-cleared all the key issues with the client. All that was left was his presentation, which would be his opportunity to display his creativity and professionalism. His stage was set, the materials were being prepared and by the end of the day, he would be "golden". He had even planned for a celebration dinner with his colleagues. He'd instructed his secretary to make reservations at one of the hottest restaurants in town and take care of all the arrangements.

It was at approximately 2:45 P.M. that day when I received a classic demonstration of how life really works. While I'd had my share of others, this one really sank in. Here's what happened.

Peter's secretary had, in fact, dutifully made all the dinner arrangements as requested. As the day progressed, she performed her tasks with her usual efficiency as her boss' anticipation of the meeting, along with his bravado, built steadily toward a crescendo.

Peter answered his own phone when the receptionist called to announce that his guests had arrived and were being seated in the conference room, and that senior management was on the way down for the meeting as well. Barely glancing her way, he barked orders for his secretary to make sure that all the copies of his presentation, which he'd instructed her to order from the copy department, were delivered to the conference room immediately.

For some reason, I looked at my watch and noticed that it was precisely 2:52 P.M. when his secretary rose from her desk, bag over her shoulder, and dropped her letter of resignation on his desk. I can still hear her words as she expressed her apology that she'd gotten so busy that she'd forgotten all about making those final corrections of his presentation, as well as ordering the copies made for his meeting. Unfortunately, however, she had an interview for a new job scheduled and had to run.

It was a stunned Peter she stood in front of that day. Some people said it was the only time in all the years they'd known him that he had no response. As she handed him the folder containing his still rough proposal, she was heard to remark, "I guess it's true. What goes around does come around, huh Peter?" I was told she said it with a distinct chuckle, though I wasn't close enough to hear.

Moments later, as word spread of the impending disaster, the phone rang and was answered by one of the other secretaries. Her voice could be heard all over the hushed board room as she called out, "Hey Peter, the restaurant is calling to confirm your reservation tonight. Is dinner still on?"

Upon retrospect, do we think that Peter even grasped his role in this debacle? We'll never know, but it's a juicy illustration of how easy it is to see in others what is so difficult to see in ourselves.

# A Thought: *Getting With the Program*

*Life works by a series of Laws*
*For the advancement of humanity*
*Which are completely supportive*
*Of any individual*
*Who acts in accordance with them*
*Nowhere in nature is there any power*
*To oppose the wishes and desires of those*
*Whose actions are in line with*
*The overall progress of life*
*For the greater good*
*The understanding of*
*And compliance with this notion*
*Is one of the common characteristics*
*Of all enduringly successful people*
*Conversely the road to misery*
*Is littered with those*
*Who for some reason*
*Just don't get it*
*In spite of the abundance*
*Of evidence showing*
*The truth of the matter*

# PREFACE: *PART I*

This book was written because over all my years out there in the business world, the arts, doing philanthropy and life in general, I have observed that while Peter may arguably be somewhat of an extreme example, there are really quite a few people who have never been taught, or if they were, at some point they came to the conclusion that it didn't apply to them, that:

*There is a direct correlation between what they spend their time and energy thinking, saying and doing, and what their quality of life turns out to be.*

I've seen people including myself, do unbelievable things and then be shocked at the subsequent turn of events, which upon reflection, was an obvious result.  I along with many, have also been surprised at a seemingly, upstanding individual's sudden turn of apparent misfortune, only to learn subsequently of actions of that individual, that clarified completely what brought that adversity their way. Thankfully, I've also had great role models like Nick, and others you'll meet.

It has been my observation, however, gleaned from a long career on Wall Street along with all the experiences attendant to career, marriage, raising children, owning homes, traveling, competing athletically, writing and performing music, creating a philanthropy and more, that:

*In spite of the continuous litany of business, sports, government and religious figures who we have seen fall from grace and receive their comeuppance, many people still do not grasp the life forces and principles at play in these cases.*

How do we know this is true? We know it because so many people continue doing different versions of the same thing that others have been taken down for. How is it possible that a professional money manager would even consider committing insider trading violations after so many have been caught? And yet offenders keep popping up. One can only conclude that they believe that where other very brilliant people have failed, they will succeed.

It is time we learned that there *are* life forces at play that explain a good deal about what happens, and that these forces are every bit as precise as the principles of gravity and electricity. It is time we learned that they *can* be understood and applied for the benefit of our overall life experience.

My perspective on these kinds of matters is somewhat unusual. I grew up with parents who were seekers of truth, attracted to the teachings of many of the great thinkers of the ages. People like Socrates, Marcus Aurelius, Meister Eckhart, Emanuel Swedenborg, Voltaire, Ralph Waldo Emerson and Albert Sweitzer were regular subjects at our dinner table. Each was an individual who looked beyond the conventional wisdom and limited thinking of their day, to discover and articulate the truth, often at the risk of great peril.

While I firmly believe that it is never too early or to late to begin the process of gaining understanding about *how life REALLY works*, I can't say it meant very much to the child who was dragged along in his parent's quest for their own personal growth. Later, however, when my life was going through a period of disarray, I began seeking my own answers. Thankfully, I knew where to turn in order to begin the journey of grasping control, and now many years later, I am still grasping, still trying and still learning.

During that time, along with family, career and all the rest, I have had the opportunity to study personally with some of the great teachers of our age. I count among them Eric Butterworth, Marianne Williamson, Raymond Charles Barker, Stuart Grayson, Louise Hay, Tom Johnson, Eric Pace, Wayne Dyer and others.

Though my tennis game may never have reached its potential and my golf skills remain minimal, I have spent countless hours studying the works of the aforementioned in addition to other great thinkers such as Emmit Fox, Donald Curtis, Charles and Myrtle Fillmore, Ernest Holmes, Phineas Parkhurst Quimby, Irwin Seale, Thomas Troward, Ralph Waldo Emerson and Joseph Campbell.

I have also had the very good fortune to be acquainted and work with people who, knowingly or not, expressed ideals worthy of striving for in their daily lives. For example...

# A Story About David

*At the time we met, David was a securities analyst with a large mutual fund company in Boston. He'd been raised in Canada, son of a prominent local businessman and had completed his education at Harvard. David was considered to be a competent professional analyst responsible for understanding the investment characteristics of companies in several industries. His job was to recommend which stocks should be purchased or sold by the various portfolio managers of his company's mutual funds.*

*The career path for someone like David was to work as an analyst for an unspecified period of time, then move into fund management which carried the ultimate buy/sell responsibility. It was in this portfolio management role that one could distinguish themselves by virtue of their documented investment track record, a challenge that David relished taking on.*

*There was no specific criteria for why and when someone would be plucked from the ranks of the analysts and be anointed, "Fund Manager". It was more a subjective judgment of the firm's top management that included investment acumen as well as personality dynamics.*

*When we crossed paths, David had been working diligently as an analyst for about ten years. Several of his peers had been promoted, but for some reason, David had not. It was beginning to look as though he might be permanently relegated to "career analyst" status, a situation that did not sit well with him.*

*He believed that he had much greater achievements within him and gradually came to the conclusion that he was unlikely to have the chance to experience them where he was, as he had hoped. He determined that for whatever reason, his superiors just did not see the personal qualities required for advancement that he knew were there. If they could not see the fire within him, he reasoned, it was time for corrective action.*

We had just completed a typically enjoyable and competitive game of tennis when David informed me of his plans. He had resolved to return to Canada and start a money-management firm of his own. His vision was to find three or four top investment pros, well-known in Canadian circles, to join him as partners in the firm. His plan was to spend weekends in Canada meeting people until he found the ones he wanted for partners, then convince them to leave their established positions and take the entrepreneurial leap with him. He would then sell his Boston house, liquidate other assets, resign from his job, and move his family to Toronto, where he would establish his business. Once that was achieved, he would then find the money for them to manage.

Listening to this extraordinary and what seemed like wildly optimistic plan exhausted me a good deal more than our game had. "How would we continue our great tennis rivalry?" I asked, among other more pertinent questions of a concerned friend.

David, however, had concluded what he would do. He was absolutely clear about it and immediately set about making it happen. Observing it as I did was a great lesson in the adage, "what mind can conceive, one can achieve."

By the time David resigned almost one year later, he had the groundwork all set for his new firm. Three prominent members of the Toronto investment community had indeed agreed to join as partners, space had been identified and a logo for the new firm's name had been created. The next day, they were in business, but the challenge had just begun.

It took over one year for David and his partners to attract their first account. During that time, he kept everyone, including himself, positive and directed. Then things started to flow. The leg work began to pay off as account after account came on board.

David kept very busy managing and building his firm. Our tennis rivalry definitely suffered, but what a tremendous achievement to watch from the sidelines. Each time we spoke, he'd update me on the amount of assets now under management. First they passed the $100 million mark, then $1 billion, then $3 billion. At last count, it was over $8 billion and growing.

*Now David can manage as much money as he wants, or spend his time foraging for new business, his favorite activity. He still has his old friends as well as many new ones he's added along the way. He's overcome the opinion and belief of others by having his own clear idea of what he wants, putting distractions aside and going after it with energy, honesty and integrity.*

*When I hear people say things like "Good guys finish last", I think of David and know instead that "what goes around comes around." In David's case, a lot of good intentions and energy went around and a lot of good in life came back.*

# A Story About Sue

*I met Sue many years ago when she had just moved to New York City to further her career as a professional artist. In fact, she had already been making a living from her painting for some time. The impetus for her move was a budding relationship with Jim, a fellow artist and a friend of mine. She moved in with him hoping that both her art and their relationship would flourish in the creative energy of New York.*

*Within a short period of time, Sue had located and set up a studio a few blocks from where she and Jim lived. She would put in long hours there every day to produce the paintings needed for her next show. The subject of them was primarily houses, large and small, one more beautiful than the next. She would work from photos taken during her travels or just from her memory. Standing in front of her canvas, she created each detail of the structure before embellishing the piece with light, flowers, fences, grass, and more, in such a manner that each one would take on a special life of its own. She told me that she never got tired of imagining the joy of the families who resided within those houses and always found motivation in the pleasure she hoped people received from having her paintings in theirs.*

*Sue had a wonderful, gentle quality and over the months, we developed a warm friendship. During one bleak period in my life, I found myself frequently at her studio door. She always welcomed me gladly and would let me sit with her while she worked, sipping a cup of tea that she prepared. Her studio, like her paintings, was full of plants and flowers. Paintings by Jim and other artist friends covered the walls. It was a magical spot of beauty, warmth and creativity. Just being there in her presence, listening to a tape of classical music or chatting quietly, bolstered my spirits and supported me through an important and difficult transition.*

In the recent past, I had gone to a showing of Sue's work, sponsored by a gallery on Madison Avenue. She had over forty paintings that she had completed over the past months on display. They ranged from small canvases of an ornate door or stained glass window, to large ones of Victorian classic homes. One in particular captivated me. It was a white beauty with a wide porch all around, offset by a lawn of deep shades of green and a picket fence. Flowers were in bloom and the bluest of skies shone above. I was drawn again and again to gaze at it for lengthy intervals. I wanted to soak it in as much as possible, while it was still free from the clutches of one of the many patrons milling about.

The price was clearly too high for the depressed state of my finances at the time and buying a painting was the furthest thing from my mind. I was there at the show out of a combination of curiosity and a desire to lend whatever support I could muster for my new friend. However, something beyond my control happened. People started buying and one after the other of her paintings were committed to. As they went, stickers indicating purchase were placed prominently on their frame. Suddenly I was compelled not to let "my special one" elude my possession. In the very moment that it was about to become the target of an avid collector of Sue's work, I leapt to make my claim. It is a decision I have never for a moment regretted. Its presence in my home over the years has provided me with countless moments of pleasure.

That show, as had most of Sue's before it, sold out and she reaped the generous rewards for the months of effort she had put into its preparation. Then, following a trip to refresh her energy and rejuvenate her creative juices, she was back at the easel to do it again. I was struck by how she was able to get herself to work every day and produce so prodigiously, with virtually no external structure or discipline imposed on her life.

"How often could you go on repeating such an arduous cycle," I wondered.

"I don't know," she answered. "To me, it's not arduous. It is simply what I do and I love it."

"Okay, but time after time you stand in front of an empty canvas. How can you be sure that you'll always be able to fill it up? What's more, how *can you know that after all the time and effort you put in, that anyone will buy it? My God, what a leap of faith!"*

*"I guess," she mused. "But honestly, I don't see why I should spend one moment or ounce of energy dwelling on it. For what? First of all, they fill themselves up. I just see them and get them started. Hey, you just bought one and I had no expectation of that. When you did, by the way, the guy you so ...umm... aggressively brushed aside, was so upset that he quickly bought two others. So, if you've got nothing else to do and want to worry about me, for me, be my guest. I'll leave it to you. By the way, I've got a great idea for this canvas. I can see it already."*

*"Gee Sue, I honestly don't know how you do it."*

*"I just paint, Rob. I just paint."*

Sue may be the greatest epitome of a purely, good person that I've ever known - zero deception – zero manipulation – pure goodness.

# A Thought: *Mysteries*

*Some are blessed*
*With clarity early on*

*Some just struggle*
*From the start*
*The road to take*
*Decisions to make*

*Why such differences*
*Nobody knows*
*Except that it's*
*A very tough call*

*Still some rise*
*From wherever they start*

*While others fall*

# Preface: *Part II*

Some years ago, deep in the search and determined to get a better handle on life, I embarked on an extensive study of principles aimed at improving all areas of life, including health, prosperity, relationships and self-expression. Why? After all, many consider the pursuit of spiritual or higher understanding to be an "other-worldly" kind of activity, reserved for those outside of the *real* world.

In fact, a study by four business school professors published in the *Journal of Business Ethics* involving nearly 400 people, found that 47% of top executives, 41% of controllers, and 76% of the graduate level business students they surveyed were willing to commit fraud by understating write-offs that cut into their companies' profits.

For myself, however, I have experienced my pursuit of greater knowledge and understanding as essential to the successful navigation of the uncharted waters of that real world. It is from this vantage point that I offer the following thoughts, gleaned from my personal, all-star team of the great thinkers of the ages, as well as my own perspective.

While many of the individuals we owe so much to were persecuted for their effort and genius, it is fortunate that the basic truth of their wisdom burned too brightly to be snuffed out. Their realizations, being basic universal principles, were likewise revealed to subsequent minds which were open and seeking truth. Thus the wisdom of the ages has continued to fight the good fight. Moreover, due to the growing prevalence of free thought and expression, the world as a whole and each individual in it, now have a golden opportunity to move to a higher level.

Much of my motivation to share these ideas derives from my understanding that lack of clarity in this area is the cause of a great deal of unnecessary misery. Some you'll soon meet certainly heaped their share upon themselves. In Nick, Peter, David and Sue, on the other hand, one can see how the way they lived their lives has resulted in either a rich tapestry of success, peace and prosperity, or the opposite. Nick, David and Sue display a natural talent for proceeding through life. They make a concerted effort to consciously stick to the *high road* – and to climb back on quickly and quietly when they slip off. The results speak for themselves, as they do for Peter.

This book's purpose is to contribute toward achieving a kind of clarification for anyone who reads it openly. It comes at a time when there is a growing outcry for a greater understanding of *how life really works*. It is part of an evolutionary process which has been going on since at least 400 BC, when Socrates roamed the streets of Athens questioning the supposed "wise men" of the day about what they thought was true and why. Fortunately, today in much of the world, one can question the precepts of authority without fear of the deadly hemlock that Socrates was condemned to drink for his so called disrespect.

Thanks to the growing prevalence of free thought, each is able to explore and study the great thinkers of history and re-purpose for ourselves the ideas that make sense. For that matter, we can also synthesize what we learn and come to our own new conclusions. We can actually improve on previously conceived ideas and add to the wisdom of the ages.

While it would be nice to think that the world was beyond the Inquisition-like impulse to torture and burn away the demons of one's blasphemy at the stake, forces of evil, such as ISIS and Boco Haram remind us how that cloud still hovers way too close for comfort.

Still, in spite of repressive forces in play, the process of *free thought* has been enabled to flourish, thanks largely to the separation of church and state pioneered by the *Founding Fathers* and adopted widely. This is true even though there is still a ways to go to engender the global peace we all hope to see in our lifetime. Having said that, nothing impedes this writer and this reader from the all-important quest for peace in our own lives.

It is an important distinction because much of history has been defined by the inter-woven power of church and governing forces, still wielded over the minds and lives of people throughout the world, and currently on full display in many of the conflicts playing out on today's world stage.

Thankfully, throughout history there have been beacons of light, individuals who were unsatisfied with the strictures and rituals of institutions. They sought their own relationship with *truth* that could empower them in every-day life. They longed for an inner peace and meaning to their existence. They questioned and pushed, and their ideas moved things along the evolutionary process of free thought. That freedom, it has been learned, carries with it the right and the responsibility of each individual to examine and think about their own individual life and what they are doing to enhance or detract from its quality.

*This right and responsibility includes giving up the shifting of blame for everything that goes wrong onto someone or something else, the acceptance of personal responsibility for the quality of one's life, and the continuing commitment to learn, evolve and grow.*

While people like David and Sue have been inspiring role models for me and others, it is not as if the act of simply observing them, in and of itself, has been sufficient for me to clone whatever they have within and claim it for myself. That is not how it works. The qualities that have enabled them to progress in life, may not easily take root in myself or others without overcoming some challenges first. We each have our own unique mix to deal with and we each have to do our own work. Nobody is living your life in your time and body but you, and of course, the same applies to us all!

There are many people however, who would rather not deal with the effort required to achieve that overcoming. They would simply prefer someone else, a priest or guru of some sort to tell them what to do. Others are turned off by the formal religions of our time. They simply can't stand any notion of morality or ethics that carries a religious connotation. Still others are just plain oblivious to the questions, not to mention answers, about life's meaning.

Having said all that, there does remain a growing urgency for answers, that has a new and different beat. It comes from the growing legions who have abandoned the myths and "legend-like" explanations of traditional philosophy and theology, along with the requirement that one suspend their intellect and simply "have faith". They want to have faith, but one backed by an understanding. They'd like to hear something that makes sense to them, without requiring them to abandon the reasoned output of their brains to do so.

This has resulted in a search for meaning which has been gathering steam and building momentum. Best sellers, such as Dr. Stephen R. Covey's, "The Seven Habits of Highly Effective People", James Redfield's, "The Celestine Prophecy", and Rhonda Byrne's "The Secret" and now this contribution, attest to this.

People want to understand *what is going on!* However, many of the traditional models just no longer apply. They have been debunked and discarded by many. Questions have been raised and answers demanded in all areas of life, including matters of career, personal relationships, health, prosperity, quality of life and more.

People today find themselves operating in a world which has been transformed dramatically in recent decades by war – sexual, racial and other revolutions – profound change in family structure, along with economic and political upheaval – ethnic ferocity and the horror of famine, disease and natural disasters. Also a general unraveling of the neat precepts and role models of the past.

We've been shocked by revelations of misdeeds by public officials, business and religious leaders, sports stars and other heroes in such a rapid fire sequence, that fiction is hard-pressed to surpass the outrageousness of factual occurrence.

Yet there are people like Nick, Sue, David, and others you'll meet in these pages and out in the real world who lead inspiring lives. They are decent yet successful, accomplished yet balanced.

The following is one of my favorites.

# A Story About Chip

*When I think of people I've known who have qualities I would like to see in my son, Courtney, Chip appears high on the list. He is devoted to his family, accomplished in his profession and active in charitable and community work. He lives according to high moral and ethical values, is an avid sports enthusiast and a terrific friend.*

*There are many specific examples I could draw from Chip's life to discuss, as his achievements are many. I'd like to focus on one, however, which involves an incident that I am sure he wishes never happened, and while he would argue that his response was anything but heroic, I disagree.*

*The incident occurred one night while Chip and his wife were heading home from a cocktail party in their new Lexus. Chip had been feeling somewhat tense as the evening began and found himself consuming an unusually large quantity of alcohol in order to relax.*

*This is not to suggest that Chip was a heavy or a regular drinker. On the contrary, for the most part, he lived a conservative and health conscious life. It was just that occasionally, he found it helpful at social events to have a few glasses of wine in order to loosen up.*

*So it was that Chip's judgment failed him as he rounded a modestly tricky curve and deposited his beautiful new car in a ditch against a large and very inhospitable rock. Thankfully, autos of such quality contain dual airbags which aquitted themselves in admirable fashion, saving Chip and his wife from more than a bent fender and the indignity of the ensuing commotion.*

*When the police arrived, Chip was cited for driving while intoxicated. He promptly lost his license for three months pending completion of a special course for DWI offenders.*

It is quite a simple matter to conclude that Chip made his own bed in this situation. It could be viewed as an excellent example of the **Law of Cause and Effect.** The way he handled it, however, was particularly impressive to me and made me prouder than ever that this terrific individual was a friend of mine.

It was early the next morning as we departed on our regular weekend run that I heard the story. "Well, I really pulled a good one," he said with a wry smile.

"Oh," I responded with characteristic brilliance.

When he completed the story, we ran along in silence for a few moments. Then I responded, "Well first of all, I'm amazed that you made it up for our run. Secondly, I'm still your friend. Third, what are you going to do now?"

"Well, there are some logistics," he answered. "I have to be in court on Monday, I'll have to take some class for a couple of months and I'll have to figure out how to get around for three months."

What a pain, I thought. How could I do it?

"The main thing is I have to do what's right for the kids," he said.

"What do you mean?" I asked.

"Well, they know what happened. They were up when we got home and know the whole story."

"So they learned you're not perfect," I said, "that won't kill them."

"That's not the point. Okay, I screwed up. What's important is how they see me handle it. I can't make a lot of dumb excuses and I have to pay the consequences in a straight-up way."

"Yea, but how can you not drive?" I asked, still not being able to comprehend that for myself. "I mean like going to the train station and running errands. I mean, you could probably still drive and just be careful. You'll never get stopped."

"Hey," he replied somewhat testily. "How can I ever tell my kids stuff about the consequences of their actions if I don't face mine fairly and squarely?

*No, it will be a pain, but I'll just have to handle it." He added, "By the way, just for the record, I'll tell you one more thing. That's the end of drinking alcohol for me. If it can put me in this kind of soup, then the heck with it. I don't need it."*

*The next three months passed quickly. Occasionally I'd hear about the woes of one of his DWI classmates, which were usually a good bit more dramatic than Chip's. He claimed to have picked up some interesting and useful thoughts from the process. Between his wife, friends, his bike and some good old-fashioned shoe-leather, Chip got around just fine with never a complaint, though I know he was relieved when the license was returned and he could put the whole incident behind him.*

Personally, I think that Chip's behavior in this matter was noteworthy and exemplary. He never tried to blame anything on anyone else. He immediately acknowledged his responsibility for the entire situation and apologized sincerely to all involved for whatever discomfort he had caused them. He chose the high road and stuck to it throughout the entire matter.

This story is certainly an example of the basic human foibles we all possess. It is also, however, the demonstration of an individual's ability to handle the very adversity they create for themselves and turn things around by grasping back control of life through exercising their power of choice in a new way.

Proud of you Chip!

# A Thought: *Credit or Blame*

Among the great things
That can occur
In one's lifetime

Is that flash of awareness
That life's highs and lows
Its goodness and badness
Its lovingness and misery

Its twists and turns in the road
Its soaring joys its darkest sadness
Belong To that one alone

There may be many
That one can think of
To thank or to blame
But there is only one
Who deserves the honor

The truth is you always
Have the same name

# The Subject of Change

One of the positive things happening is a renewed interest in figuring things out in a manner that makes sense in the context of contemporary life. This book addresses one particular aspect of the search for that understanding. That is – what exactly makes things happen the way they do in life? In other words:

*How Does Life REALLY Work?*

It may seem like a basic enough question, but for some reason the answer isn't so straightforward. In fact, I have personally observed some of the smartest people I have known engage in the kind of misery-producing activities that prove conclusively, that they had no idea how life works. That is not to mention my own personal blunders. However, even when the truth is right in front of one's nose, actual behavioral change in the real world, under the pressure of events taking place, is extremely difficult for any person. Yet, it is true that:

*"The only way life can change for you, is for
you to change how you handle life."*

There are many prescriptions or road maps for how to change, but no matter which a person may attempt to follow, success always comes down to the individual's willingness and ability to *actually perform the change*. Furthermore, no person can do it for anyone else. Rather, each person's challenge is doing it for themselves, and unless there is a deep grasp of why it is important, essential, and crucial to do so, making these changes borders on the impossible.

Not that it's all that complicated. On the contrary, most of the very important ideas in life are really quite rudimentary and easy to understand conceptually. On some level, we all know them. They are in some cases, however, a daunting challenge to consistently put in practice, particularly when life is presenting us with attractive reasons to ignore them.

In my case for example, I have been exposed to the ideas described herein for many years. One would think they would have sunken in by now and I'd be firmly in control of myself. Ha! Rather, I continue to blunder along because I either forget them in the moment of truth, or just plain have difficulty applying what I know, when it counts.

I am reminded of the poem, *"There's a Hole in My Sidewalk"*, by Portia Nelson. It describes a woman who continually walks down a particular road, and each time falls into the exact same hole. At first, she doesn't see this hole that she keeps falling into. Eventually, she notices the hole, but still keeps falling in. At last, triumphantly, she sees the hole and walks around it, then takes another road! Hurray!!!

This just highlights the question of why is it so often the case, that we require multiple blows to the head to get the point?

I call it *the fog descending*, when I find myself doing, saying, or thinking something that I know perfectly well is not supportive of my own objectives. It is my version of falling into the hole, yet again, a kind of personal sabotage. Thankfully, I have occasionally noticed the hole. More and more I do catch myself in the moment of truth and apply what I know. But I'd be less than honest to suggest that I've overcome all of my personal examples of *the hole*. The point is that one never stops learning, should never stop trying and never stop reminding ourselves. Who knows, the next time might just be the one that works.

The title of this book, *"What goes Around Comes Around,"* is a phrase we have all used and understand intuitively. The subtitle and theme is *How Life REALLY Works*, which is obviously extremely important for everyone and anyone to get a grip on. Yet it remains broadly misunderstood.

It is precisely this condition that over the centuries has allowed various religions, philosophies, disciplines, charismatic leaders, cults, etc., to fill the breach for those who sincerely desired answers, but for some reason found comfort in having those answers defined for them by an entity outside of themselves, regardless of what their common sense may have told them.

It is apparent that many elements of society, business, government, and other, consider the concern about these issues to be a *nice to have* rather than a *need to have* matter. A matter of *convenience* rather than one of *necessity*. There is a good reason for this misperception. The fact is that even with signs clearly posted and red flags all around:

*It is challenging at best, to see the direct linkage in one's world, between one's own thoughts, words and actions and the subsequent quality of that one's life.*

This is so even though you can often see it clearly in the lives of others. It is a conundrum – a challenging subject to present clearly or to grasp, and even more difficult to apply in principle. The fact is, however, that the specific way life works plays a very central and practical role in your life and mine, whether we are aware of it or not:

*Lack of awareness makes life appear to be a series of disconnected incidents caused by luck, circumstance and whim. Awareness removes the mystery and begins the process of placing control directly in the hands of each individual.*

This book strives to build that awareness about *how life REALLY works*. It is about building deeper awareness of how it impacts you and those closest to you. Over the centuries of life on this planet, many others have written and spoken about the same concepts, which is okay. More than that, it's good! It is affirmative and validating. But even though the same things may have been said countless times to countless people, they've never been said by this person, and read by you before. So here goes with a story about JRT, but first...

# A Thought: *Laws of Nature*

*Nature is nature*
*Whether dealing with*
*It's incredible balance and gravity*
*Or for that matter human beings*

*In some instances the rules of the game*
*Are less obvious than others*
*But they are always as precise*
*As the saying goes, don't mess with Mother*

*At one point all have observed*
*The folly of challenging laws of nature*
*Though some are more subtle*
*Than others to discern*

*When this is the case*
*There are those who are tempted*
*To display mindless behavior*
*Thinking no one can see*
*Then be surprised by the results*

*The truth is bad things happen*
*When lower selves prevail*
*The good part is that*
*The opposite is also true*

# A Story About JRT

When I met JRT, he was by most standards, already a great success. He'd grown up in a poor immigrant family in a deteriorating neighborhood of an old and crumbling industrial city. He graduated from the State University, the first in his family to graduate from college and began his career as a stockbroker with a well-known Wall Street firm. JRT was the pride of his family and community. He started in the firm's home office in NYC, developing business back in his home state. He did so well that he was soon moved back to work in a branch office in the financial center of that state.

JRT worked diligently, calling on corporate treasurers, wealthy individuals and professional money managers, standing out in his peer group as an up and coming producer. Every few weeks, he would get in his car for the two hour drive on the interstate to visit his family. During these visits, he was reminded of the tremendous gap between where he came from and the world he was breaking into.

It would get to him at times, when he thought about the family background, education and cultural exposure that many of his clients had, which in his mind, he had missed out on. He felt deep down, considering his so-called inferior background and educational credentials that it would be extremely difficult for him to ever win their true respect as a professional equal, as long as he was in the position of calling on them for business. The only solution, he concluded, was to start a money management firm of his own and become one of them.

Within a year of his decision, JRT had the necessary commitments to take the plunge, starting with about $30 million under management. He had a real talent for investing and his good record started to attract attention. He began being invited to compete for business against other more *established managers, the kind who had the credentials, education, etc. that he so envied.*

*At times, in the heat of the battle, he found himself exaggerating little bits of his background to make up for what he perceived to be his competitive shortcomings. He won enough times so that his firm grew steadily over the years. When I met him, he had twelve employees and managed about $600 million. He'd also had the opportunity to participate in some venture capital investments which paid off in a big way for him and his clients. Everything seemed to be working.*

*For JRT, however, something was still wrong. When he'd go out to restaurants or meetings where other investment managers were present, he would receive, at best, polite acknowledgment. He was as successful as many of them and still growing, but he still felt out of place. In JRT's mind, he was definitely not, "in the club." In his view, his blood was just not the right shade of blue and never would be.*

*It struck JRT that if he was ever going to achieve the recognition he wanted, it would have to be on a different stage. He concluded that his personal narrative, where he came from and what he'd achieved, could possibly work in politics, i.e. – poor local boy who makes it in business, now wants to give something back. Soon after, JRT announced his intention to run for the Republican gubernatorial nomination, to challenge the incumbent Democratic governor, and initiated a vigorous campaign around the state.*

*"What the state needed to cure its many problems," he said, "was a successful businessman who wasn't handed life on a silver plate – someone who understood how things really worked, but who also understood the needs of common people."*

*It was an effective pitch and JRT was a passionate and compelling speaker. Before long, he was leading his competition for the nomination by a wide margin in all the polls. Yet at the same time, this undertaking was being viewed with a highly skeptical eye by the investment community, which for some reason, had never come to feel like they could trust this guy. To many, he just didn't seem genuine.*

JRT's campaign was picking up steam and he was actually starting to draw national media attention. Then the soup hit the fan. Days before the state primary election, the local newspaper ran a lead headline story about discrepancies it had found in some of JRT's campaign literature. Things that were claimed in some of his mailing pieces, which background checks had proven to be fabrications. He issued statements claiming them to be innocently overlooked mistakes of his campaign manager, which in the whirlwind of the campaign, he had failed to catch.

The damage was done, however. He lost the primary badly, which had been virtually his for the taking. Recent polls had even shown him to be a real threat to the incumbent. His worst nightmares, however, could not have anticipated the reaction of the investment community. He became an instant pariah and laughingstock. Then, as if things weren't bad enough, a number of his firm's investors, remembering the exaggerations of his original presentations, now proven bogus, pulled their money from his firm.

Some of the issues in question had actually been correctly represented. Unfortunately for JRT, several had not been. His campaign manager was a long-standing colleague who had heard JRT's lies for so long that he'd assumed they were true and included them in his biographic campaign material. For some reason, JRT either didn't pay attention to what went into the material, as he claimed, or just couldn't bring himself to admit, even to his close associate, that these claims had better be left out of his biography.

Fortunately for JRT, he had personally made substantial profits, as he'd done for his clients, thanks to his investment prowess. However, dreams and career shattered, he felt compelled to move his family to another city to escape the glare and start over as a private investor.

# A Thought: *Whence the Grade?*

*The test*
*That matters*

*Is not what you*
*Turn out*

*At the end*
*Of the day*

*To be*
*Grateful for*

*The true test*
*Is how many others*

*Have even*
*The slightest reason*

*To be grateful*
*That in their life*

*Is you*

# A Story About Ben

*By contrast, Ben was one of the best people I've ever known. He was a wonderful husband, father, grandfather and friend. He had a successful small town law practice, and over the years, came through for many people, in tough times, including me. There are two particular cases of his kindness to me, that I will never forget. They were instrumental in shaping my own views and behavior when confronted with an opportunity to assist someone else in a time of need.*

*As with many others over the years, I got to know Ben through tennis. Although we were a rather unlikely pair because of our age difference, we became tennis partners and great friends. For a certain period of time, we played together as a team, two or three times a week. Actually, Ben's wife Audrey and my mother were close personal friends from their volunteer work with the Girl Scouts. Their two kids were both older than I am. Still, while in my twenties, Ben and I began a friendship that would last for quite a few years, until he passed away.*

*Playing tennis with Ben was always a lesson in tenacity and good sportsmanship. He was a fierce competitor, yet he never said a negative word about any of my bone-headed mistakes or ill-advised shots. "Good try" or "too bad" was all I'd hear him utter. Following a heads-up play or winning shot, I could always count on an, "Oh, that was a great shot," type of comment.*

*Afterwards, when recounting the game to Audrey, or whoever happened to be within earshot, Ben would proudly describe my outstanding play, tenacity and never-say-die attitude. To listen to him, one would think that I was almost ready for "The Tour." Banished into oblivion were those overheads into the net or the back fence, double faults on game point and other misadventures of my game.*

*Overall we actually did pretty well in the playground circuit of our community. I knew, however, that when playing with Ben I somehow seemed to play just a little better than I really was. It was also the most fun. Oh sure, we got down when we'd lose, but that would end as quickly as the next match began. Once on the court, we did our best and just had fun.*

*Something I noticed about Ben was that wherever we played, people always seemed to know him and like him. He was always friendly and pleasant to everyone he met and never questioned or chastised an opposing player's call. I observed that players who would normally question and berate other opponents, would never say a word to Ben. They just couldn't. He was simply too great a competitor and too decent a person to be nasty to. It was an interesting revelation and I've done my best to emulate him.*

*Shortly before he died, Ben and I got together for a game. He'd been in and out of the hospital with severe health problems including muscle atrophy in his legs, and hadn't played in over a year. My life had taken me away for a while as well, so we hadn't been together for quite some time. When I picked him up, he was cheerful as ever and we chatted enthusiastically on the way to the park, catching up on each other's lives. When we arrived at the courts, there was a chorus from the regulars. "Hey Ben, how ya doin'?" "Hey Ben, come over and play with us!" "Oh no, the bulldog is back," got a particularly big smile from him.*

*We had great fun that day. He could barely walk, so I did a lot of running around. There he was though, out there having a great time, imparting "good try's," and "too bad's," and "hey, there's a great shot," and playing his heart out as always. We sat together talking for a long time after we finished playing... about four sets later!*

*Though I regrettably missed his funeral and the gathering of family and friends afterward. I would have loved to have been there to pay tribute to one of the best human beings I have ever known. I learned afterward, not surprisingly, that the outpouring of love from all over the country was stunning, for he had affected many in the same manner he did me. I heard that his son gave a profound and touching eulogy. I know that his family's love for him was as strong and deep as his for them. His wife misses him greatly, his warmth and optimism, his cheerfulness and strength. We all do. I think of him often.*

I wonder sometimes what I am doing to plant the kind of seeds he did. I wonder what my son will say when I am gone, whether my children will miss me? I wonder what sort of value I am creating through my thoughts and words and actions. I think my friend Ben was in a league of his own. I, like many, am still just working on getting into a league.

# The Time Factor

This may be the most important part of this entire effort as it addresses the vexing question of why it appears that many people never get caught or punished for their evil doings? It is the question that messes the most with people's minds when it comes to getting their arms around accepting the premise of this book, that *"What goes Around Comes Around."*

Why, they may rightfully ask, is it true that in nature when a seed is planted, it is very precise when the bloom will appear. But in the human experience in which the *seeds* planted are thoughts, words, and actions, the rightful consequences may take a very long time to appear, or even seemingly never appear? Why aren't humans, it can logically be asked, subject to the same laws of nature as all other living creatures?

Let's go straight to it! Is it true that some people can get away with doing bad things without being subjected to appropriate consequences? It's not like this is the first time this question has ever been posed. Not at all. It is one of those universal stumpers that have plagued humankind from our inception. So its not surprising that it should still be doing so now.

There are teachings, ancient and more recent which surmise that the consequences for a person's actions in this life may not appear until the next lifetime, or that they will be *visited* upon the perpetrator's children and their children. Whoa! Going there is way too esoteric for this treatise, which is solely concerned with is what happens in *this* lifetime!

Though it must be acknowledged that this is one of those questions that no living being, now or ever, truly knows the answer to, the clearest and most cogent explanation I've ever found, comes from the person many consider to be the greatest poet and philosopher in America's history, Ralph Waldo Emerson. It was in reading his magnificent essay on *Compensation* that I had my first glimpse of how the issue at hand works. It resonated with me and was very helpful in formulating the views expressed herein. He states:

- "Though no checks to a new evil appear, the checks exist, and will appear."

- "Every secret is told, every crime is punished, every virtue rewarded, every wrong redressed, in silence and certainty!"

- "The retribution is inseparable from the thing, but is often spread over a long time, and so may not become distinct until much time has passed. However, the offense and the punishment grow out of one stem. Cause and Effect, Means and Ends, Seeds and Fruit, cannot be severed, for the Effect already blooms in the Cause."

- "Life invests itself with inevitable conditions, which the unwise seek to dodge, or say they do not know, or that they do not touch them. But they do!"

These are all tidbits of Emersonian, philosophical, insight. However, still missing is the why? Emerson and others have readily observed that much water can flow under the bridge before a wrong gets righted. But why?

The answer lies hidden right beneath our noses, out of view in plain sight. It is so simple, yet as it relates to this issue, we just don't see it, and miss the truth right in front of us. What I speak of is the very quality that makes humans different from all other living creatures, namely the *gift of choice!* This is not a subject that any one of us has never heard about, talked about or exercised as their freedom to make choices. We think about what to do and then do it. We say, "I choose to go to the beach, or the bar, or out dancing or to bed early.

It is this very significant ability to make choices that provide us with the facility to go with or against the crowd, the gift to chart our own course regardless of the opinions and beliefs of others, to break the limited thinking and boundaries that others erect and want to control us with, or importantly, to choose not to do so. We call it a gift, a good thing, a blessing, a privilege, and properly employed that is true!

But there is another side to it. Having the ability to choose -- freedom of choice -- also means that one can choose to use that gift to lie and misdirect, to deceive and obfuscate, to use one's intelligence, charm and cleverness to do everything possible to put off the consequences of the seeds they've planted, to some future time.

Emerson says, *the offense and the punishment grow out of the same stem, but the retribution may be spread over time.* That's right! There's your answer! Some people are just better than others – more clever at covering their tracks – scarier at intimidating witnesses – more able to pay people off.

*Just like every other skill or sport or art form, there are infinite gradations of ability that people have or cultivate to achieve their goal. Watch twenty-five different TED talks, and you'll see twenty-five different levels of speech-making ability. Why would lying and cheating be any different. It is also true that only humans have the ability to take duplicity to levels we could never expect, and as we repeatedly witness in crystal clarity, many do!*

Yes, its true that people can use their intelligence and freedom to make their own choices and maneuver away from consequences for some indeterminate period of time, depending on their level of skill. But the iron rule is, that whether entertainment figure, clergy, sports hero, professor, doctor, elected official or some other brand of villain, the longer they obfuscate, lie, cheat and evade, the deeper the hole that they dig for themselves. We'll explore this further in a moment.

There's no question that it is very difficult and disconcerting to know someone who does bad things, particularly if it's personal and you have felt the sting, to wholly accept the idea that *what goes around comes around.* Emerson tells us that the retribution is inseparable from the thing, but is often spread over a long time frame.

In fact, we are living through a period in which retribution after many years of offending behavior is on display everywhere we look. Events are confirming that every wrong is rectified in its apparently, appropriate time frame.

Further that the factor differentiating one time frame from another is the talent of the offender to hide out in the shadows for a shorter or longer period than some other villain. But as suggested earlier, when the light shines and the shadow disappears, all is revealed, including *how deep the pit.*

To think about that in another way, consider these examples:

Example 1 - You and I have just met and you are in the middle of explaining something about yourself that is obviously important to you. Suddenly and without warning, I turn and walk away from you without an explanation, leaving you dumbfounded as to what just happened. A few minutes later, someone approaches you and asks,

*"Hey I saw you speaking to that guy Rob Davis. What kind of a person is he?"*

What are you likely to say? Probably at best it would be something like,

*"Well we just met and I don't really know him. Can't give you much insight."*

But at worst, you might say,

*"The guy's a real jerk. Stay away from him!"*

Now suppose that moments after walking away, I come back to you and say,

*"Oh gosh, I'm so sorry. Just as we were starting to speak, I saw someone I needed to give an urgent message to, and have been trying to reach for days. But my goodness, that was so rude of me to just walk away like that without an explanation. I'm really sorry. Can you please let me off the hook for that. Could we just start that conversation over again? Honestly, I'm really interested in what you were saying?"*

Our conversation goes on for 15-20 minutes and ends with our agreement to meet for lunch the following week. Now that same person comes over to you and asks,

*"Hey, I saw you speaking to that guy Rob Davis. What kind of person is he?"*

What are you likely to say now? Probably something quite different from the last example, and that difference would have hinged on the decision I made to come back to you and correct my blunder.

What if I had not done that and had just left it to fester, and you were asked your opinion about me say a month, or six months, or a year later. Would your opinion of me have improved? Not likely! Probably the opposite. Left unaddressed, it most likely would have festered and deteriorated further with time, not improved.

But in this example, I did correct it and was able by doing so, to minimize the damage that could have been caused by my mindlessness. Of course, if I were to do it again...not good! It would be much more difficult to repair the next time. So it goes...

*Immediately addressed, even problematic issues can be, at least to some extent, resolved. It's the choice of the perpetrator of the offending action, to either mitigate their blunder or not. The longer it takes, the deeper the pit they dig for themselves.*

The point of view taken here is that there are always consequences, whether visible to the world at large or not. They may be subtle and not readily discernible at the moment.

However as Ralph Waldo observed, "...the checks are there, and will appear."

Example 2 - Bernie Madoff - By all accounts, Bernie had a successful, established, securities trading and market making business, before he embarked on the path that led to his ruin, and that of many others including loved ones and close associates. It was some time after he began accepting money to manage from outside investors that the wheels fell off his performance statistics and he could not bring himself to admit it.

Because I did not know Bernie and was never able to corroborate it first hand, I am speculating when I say this, but my guess is that he could not accept what in his mind must have meant humiliation. Instead he covered it up with accounting chicanery, probably thinking that he'd be able to make up the performance in future quarters with no one the wiser.

But it didn't work out like that. Instead I surmise, it got worse, and before he knew it he was on the slippery slope of being the progenitor of a full-fledged *ponzi scheme*. Old investors now had to be paid off or redeemed, with the money coming in from new investors. It can work as long as there is a steady stream of those new investors providing the cash flow to keep the deception alive.

It also requires nobody seeing through it sufficiently to blow the whistle. But once that window closes...game over! It was certainly one of the most successful and long-lived such criminal ventures of any before, reportedly lasting more than twenty years.

Now in his 70's, both of Madoff's sons are dead, his wife has lived through hell, he's lost everything that meant so much to him including that reputation, and he will be restricted to a prison cell for the rest of his life. Not to mention, that unless they change it, his grandchildren will carry that name and forever be asked *the question!*

But just suppose, just imagine, that following that first fateful three month quarter when things went wrong with his performance, that Bernie had scheduled a conference call with all his investors and other interested parties and come clean. What if he'd fessed up to his failure, asked to be forgiven and offered to make full restitution?

If he had done that, what would his penalty have been? Maybe a fine? He probably would have been forced to shut that business down which would have saved many much misery, most of all him! But there's a chance he may have been forgiven, embraced and given a clean slate.

What if he had done that after six months? After a year? In each case the answer would have been harsher, but nothing compared to the what actually happened. Why? Because freedom of choice, the thing that differentiates humans from all other living creatures, also provides a "space in time" for people to either do the "right" thing, or not – for them to be honest or to continue perpetuating a lie, as Bernie did!

Could Madoff have taken the high road, the path of acknowledging his very human, screw-up, of poor investment returns? It is the same screw-up that legions of professional money managers have made before and since. Of course he could have. He could have because as we have been taught, human beings are the only living creatures on the earth that have freedom of choice.

Instead, Bernie's conscious choice was to obfuscate. It was to create an elaborate and complex deception. To lie and steal. He was incredibly good at it, a testament to his intelligence. If only he'd used that intellect for the good of humanity rather than for all the pain it wrought. What would have been the outlook for his family and loved ones then? For himself?

So it is that this gift bestowed upon humans, the one that provides free choice, comes with what Emerson would refer to as:

*"The equally, counter-balancing responsibility to use that freedom the right way."*

So it also is that this very freedom of choice can postpone the eventual reckoning, due to the many nuances of decisions that clever and intelligent people have within their power of choice to make. However, for those who get upset with how long some people seem to get away, I hope you'll get some comfort now from knowing that, the longer they do, the deeper the pit!

It all comes crashing down when those choices no longer work. That happened to Bernie Madoff when the financial crisis of 2008 descended and choked off that cash flow he so depended on. It was only then that he was forced to confess to his family and the world what he'd done.

Only then was he forced to suffer the most extreme of all possible humiliations, a downfall of unprecedented proportion from revered to reviled, called a monster, and convicted to prison for the rest of his life.

He had free choice to either make corrections or to dig as deep as possible for as long as possible. He chose to keep digging, and digging, and digging.

Another nuanced twist that plays havoc with many folk's perceptions of the title's veracity is when the case at hand is highly personal. An example is when one person is wronged by another but does not have the resources to get that person back, and see them suffer in kind.

In a situation like that, the offended person might not believe that the title is more than a nice platitude that may sometimes be true, but is not a law of nature every bit as precise as the law of gravity, because they were not able to bring about one on one retribution, witness it first hand, or learn about it from some other source.

It is a challenge for many to accept is that its not a one on one matter, and there's no need for their guts to churn. There is no need because if the offender was underhanded in their actions, they will, like night follows day, get theirs in equal measure. If it doesn't come directly from the aggrieved, it will be from some other source at some other time. Something will happen in that person's life that will, without question, balance the ledger. Yet it can be a challenge to know and believe that is the case.

It can save much agony though, to know that there is a *Law of Life* that does the work. The offender, in committing a lowly act toward another, has planted a very nasty seed in their garden of life that some point in time, is going to show up as equally nasty and strangulating weeds blocking their good and punishing them in some way.

Neither the offended one or the offender may ever know the specific connection, or the aggrieved may hear way later about something that has happened to the offender, and not realize it is payback for what happened to them. Or, they may never hear about it, but it will happen, nonetheless.

This is not to suggest that a person who has been cheated, or lied to, or treated badly in some other way should not take steps to protect or defend themselves. It just means they need not agonize if they don't get personal retribution. Nor for that matter should they think that they are the only ones this person has negatively treated. More likely, there are multiple victims and the natural laws of life are already closing in.

Moreover, perhaps the most important point to not lose sight of, is what seeds you yourself are planting in your own garden of life. Seething resentment, hatred, and a churning gut have no effect on their target, only on you — and it's not a good effect. But knowing that person will get theirs no matter what you do or don't do? Now that is a much more healthy way to go.

In fact, I can hear my very wise Nana saying, "Dear boy, no matter how low another may stoop, never let them make you go there with them. They are going to have to pay *out* of their proverbial pocket for their actions. Make sure you get paid *into* yours!"

That's how it works, and that's why it sometimes appears that people get away with bad things. Don't worry, they're not. They're just digging that pit deeper for themselves.

There are countless other examples we could use to illustrate this issue of *"The Time Factor."* Another good one is Raj Rajaratnam, the evil founder and Chief Investment Officer of The Galleon Hedge Fund. He was convicted to the longest sentence of the hundred plus investment managers, analysts and others convicted of insider trading over the past few years.

I use the descriptor "evil," because of the way Raj charmed and tempted and drew weaker people he deemed could be useful to him, into his web of deceit. Of course, those others made their choices and suffered their consequences, but Raj is a perfect example of why there is such confusion about "The Time Factor" discussed earlier.

Anyone who knew how Raj was cheating, and had been for years, would have said, "See, the bad guys get away with their deception and get all the rewards. It's not fair, but it's just the way it is!" They would have said that, it should be clarified, until October 13, 2011 when Rajaratnam was sentenced to eleven years in prison.

Then there are the druggie athletes whose covers have been blown, the sexual predators in business, government, entertainment, sports and elsewhere; all revealed to have abused their positions of influence or power over others.

And now, in the most stunning, alarming and despicable revelation of all, the abuse of thousands of children, by more than 300 priests, over a period of 70 plus years, brought to light by a Grand Jury investigation of accusations of abuse in the state of Pennsylvania.

The cover-up over all those years included the corruption of public officials in exchange for votes. It had the long-standing, highly cultivated and sophisticated effectiveness, that would be the envy of any criminal enterprise in history. We'll no doubt be watching the *effect* side of this debacle play out for some time – *"the checks are there and will appear."*

These examples, all tell the same story, and say what they might, the fact is that whatever the consequences may be, the perpetrators will have brought them on entirely by themselves. Nobody held a gun to their heads to hurt others and be criminals. They just didn't believe it. They didn't think it was true that...

*"What Goes Around Comes Around."* They also thought it was just a platitude.

Yes, they are all good demonstrations of the principles discussed herein, but tune in now for a real barn burner!

# A Story About Eliot Spitzer

*The Eliot Spitzer Story – or – where else could Eliot have been?*

*This is a story about Eliot Spitzer, the former Attorney General and Governor of New York State. It is a true tale that relates to the incidents that brought Eliot down from the heights he had achieved as the elected Governor of NY State. However, this part of the story has never been told before and relates to why his fall was so sudden, so brutal and so far. I am one of only three people, the others being Eliot and a staff member, who know the true circumstances surrounding that self-destructive night, the one that took Eliot from the brink of political stardom to the depths of infamy. I've never told this story before publically, but have decided to do so here, because of the good I hope it will do by helping to drive home the importance and truth presented in these pages.*

*I have thought extensively about whether I should reveal this story, and if so, how to do it. In the immediate aftermath, and trauma it put his family through, it felt like piling on. So, for these past years I've kept it to myself. I felt that Eliot and his family had enough to survive without me making it worse. I also knew (see the title of this book) that if I did reveal it for the wrong reasons, such as out of my personal pique, or to make myself look clever in some way, that it would most likely do me more harm than good.*

*However, now seems to be the time. Years have passed – the tale sits squarely in the context of this book – and it constitutes an important object lesson about the book's primary purpose, namely gaining insight toward understanding how life really works! With one exception, this book's message is conveyed by stories about people I have known, including Eliot. My hope is that this telling helps drive home a critical idea about the power of our thoughts, words and actions to shape the life that we subsequently experience.*

*How often have you heard someone say, "Well, I only thought the thought, I didn't do the deed. No harm, no foul, right?" Perhaps you've said the same thing! Ummm…no…not so fast. The fact is, that every one of our thoughts, words and actions is a seed we plant in our garden of life, and sure as the sun rises and sets each day, it will, at some point, come up to greet us. In fact, a potent remedy for misery taught by great teachers and philosophers throughout the ages is to cultivate the discipline and awareness to carefully "select" the seeds we plant.*

*Now back to Eliot. Without going into all the details of how it came about, suffice it to say there was a period of time during his New York Attorney General days, when I was on a somewhat friendly basis with Eliot, and his wife Silda. It goes back to 2005, when as the Founder and Chairman of Hedge Funds Care - Help for Children, I invited Eliot to be the Keynote Speaker at our annual gala benefit, held in February at the Marriott Marquis Hotel in Times Square.*

*At the time it was a controversial choice to say the least, because as Attorney General, Eliot had taken on certain Wall Street business practices. He'd become known as the "Sheriff of Wall Street" by uncovering conflicts of interest that resulted in large fines for brokerage firms and changes in those practices. But I had seen him in action and knew what a great speaker he was. When he went to the podium he caught everyone by surprise. His speech was charming, gracious and funny. As the father of three girls, he said how moved he was by the charity's mission of preventing child abuse and providing treatment to those who have been victimized. He talked about the things he had done as AG to protect children and bring perpetrators to justice. Within moments he had the audience of 1,000 plus people applauding. When the speech was over, he was acknowledged by a standing ovation and I received many compliments for having the audacity and courage to invite him.*

*Shortly after the benefit Eliot wrote me the following letter:*

Dear Rob,

Needless to say, it was my pleasure to have the opportunity to participate in the Hedge Funds Care "Open Your Heart To The Children Benefit." Congratulations to you for starting such an incredible organization. I am delighted that it was such a success.

I look forward to seeing you again in the near future. Warmest regards.

Sincerely,
Eliot

*The following year, with much support from Wall Street, Eliot was elected as the 54th Governor of New York State. During that interval we stayed in touch and I attended political fundraisers arranged for him. We had breakfast meetings and I attended events for Silda's charity, "Children For Children". When he was elected Governor we had a long conversation and over the months several more. Then came the summer of 2007.*

*On a scorching July evening, I attended another charity event I'd been invited to at Chelsea Pier. It was not until I arrived that I learned that Eliot was the keynote speaker. I was a bit late arriving and he was already at the podium delivering his comments. I can't say what it was he discussed that evening but I do recall vividly what happened after.*

*I was standing to the side of the podium watching Eliot when I felt a hand on my arm. It was Silda. She had spotted me and come over to say hi. She pulled me near the steps where Eliot would come down from the podium when he finished his speech. When he was done and spotted us, he waved as he made his way through all the well wishers. It was in that moment that I had an inspiration.*

*When he reached us he gave me a hug and right away asked, "How's that Hedge Funds Care doing?"*

*"Great," I said, "And funny you should ask! Eliot, now you're the Governor and next year will be our tenth anniversary. Would you consider coming*

back to be our keynote speaker once again?" Then I looked right at Silda shaking my head up and down to get her agreement, and said, "And this time bring Silda and the girls?"

Silda laughed and said, "That's right Eliot! Last time you went without us. It would be good for the girls to be there with us and see their Dad working for such a good cause.

Eliot laughed too and asked for the date. February 13th, 2008, I told him.

"Should be ok", he said." He handed me a card and wrote his direct office number and the name of his scheduling assistant on it."Tell him we had this conversation and that I said to block that date off. I'll make sure it happens."

"Terrific!" I responded, ecstatic at my good fortune to have run into Eliot and Silda.

Mainly I was thrilled to have the issue of keynote speaker at our next benefit all settled so early in the process. I looked forward to being able to report that the speaker at our next gala would be the Governor of New York State. It was all so light-hearted and pleasant that I never could have expected what happened next.

The "Committee of Hearts" is the volunteer group that comes together each year to sell sponsorships to our big annual shindig which is called, "The Open Your Heart To The Children Benefit". They were working away on filling seats and bragging that we'd have Eliot there to give his State of the State and latest zingers about Wall Street, when I received "the" note.

It was dated January 23, 2008, and came from a person with the title Director, Executive Chamber operations. The note said:

> Dear Mr. Davis,
>
> Governor Spitzer has asked me to thank you for inviting him to attend the 10th Annual Hedge Funds Care benefit. He is honored by your request that he be part of this special event, so needless to say, he is disappointed that his schedule

prevents him from accepting. We have no doubt, however, that it will be a great success.

Once again, thanks you for your kind invitation. Your thoughtfulness is greatly appreciated.

> Warmest regards,
> Sincerely,
> *(Signature omitted to protect the guilty)*

*That was not a nice note to receive. It was barely three weeks before the event and Eliot was cancelling something he had agreed to six months before. Plus we had made a big deal out of the fact that he was going to be there. But what could be done? We needed to make sure that the morale of the troops remained high, since we were already facing another enormous challenge, the worst financial crisis in our lifetime. With many of our important supporters on the ropes, we really could have used Eliot's promised support.*

*You can surely see that it wasn't a good time for this head fake from Eliot. But I also had to face up to the question, what was my responsibility in this? Maybe it was that I'd been complacent and had over-estimated my quote "friendship" with Eliot and was now paying the price for that. I had certainly been proud, obviously overly so of the fact that I'd been able to line up, "my good friend the Governor." Hey check me out. Aren't I important?*

*To be truthful, when I received the note, I was at least as disappointed that it did not come from Eliot himself, as the fact that he wasn't coming. Wow, I thought at the time. he doesn't even give me a call, or write the note himself! I guess that shows where I rank on his totem pole!*

*Of course, that was my private lament. Publicly, the important work of making sure the event was successful quickly took precedence and nose went to the grindstone. Thankfully, by this time in the life of the organization, Hedge Funds Care had strong leadership beyond me and many highly committed individuals who threw themselves into the fray. Somehow, we held it together and survived.*

*I can't say the same for Eliot.*

*On March 10, 2008 it was revealed in the New York Times that Eliot had been caught through wire taps, arranging to spend the night of February 13 – yes – the night of our gala, with a high-priced prostitute at a Washington, DC, hotel. Further, that because he had paid for her to travel across state lines, the charges could be very serious. The investigation also showed that far from being a one-time event, Eliot had been hiring such services for years. This was so even though he had often boasted about prosecuting others – a real head scratcher.*

*We have all heard so many fall-from-grace stories over past years that to some degree we've become numb to the shock. Even so, Eliot's was something! A guy, who as the top cop in NYC had pursued and prosecuted crimes of all sorts, including prostitution, was now on the other side.*

*For one thing, how could he have put himself into such a position? How many times did we say or hear the words, "What was he thinking?" Consider also, what must it have felt like to learn that he'd been nailed with the same investigative techniques that he had used so many times himself to get the "bad guys," of which he was now officially one!*

*One day Governor of New York State, the next day the object of scorn and ridicule. He was forced to resign or potentially face serious criminal charges. It was a fall as stunning and precipitous as they come. And what I knew, that was unknown by almost anyone else at the time, was that Eliot had not only made the choice everyone knew about, but also the following:*

*Rather than:*

> *Stay at home in New York City; Take his wife and three daughters to the Hedge funds Care "Open Your Heart To The Children Benefit," with the mission of funding programs dedicated to saving children from the trauma of abuse; Give the Keynote address with his family looking on, to an audience of people all gathered for*

*that noble purpose; Then take his family home, tuck his daughters in, exchanging hugs and kisses good-night.*

Eliot chose:

> *Arrange a surreptitious liaison with a professional hooker in the nation's capital under the guise of attending a crucial meeting; Initiate machinations to hide the transfer of funds to pay her fee; Engage in the very same deception that he pursued and prosecuted as a member of the Manhattan District Attorney's office and the State Attorney General of New York; Leave his wife and three daughters at home.*

Wow, what a choice! Nothing much else to say.

# A Thought: *Action / Reaction*

*Why is it*
*That some people*
*Would never think*
*Of going swimming in a lightning storm*

*But think nothing*
*Of berating their spouse*
*Or a child*

*Or to cheat on an expense account*
*Or their taxes*

*To undermine a colleague*
*Or lie to a friend*

*They must think*
*These kinds of actions*
*Disappear harmlessly*
*Into the air*

*That nothing happens*
*In response to them*

*That these kinds of things*
*Will generate*
*No reciprocal action*
*That may*
*Return to them in kind*

*Big mistake*

# THE TITLE – WHAT IT MEANS

The phrase from yesteryear was, *"As You Sow, So Shall You Reap."* It was an expression that was common wisdom at the time. Because so many people have become turned off to religious-sounding jargon, however, when we hear a statement like this, it can easily push the tune-out button, dismissed as just another esoteric concept with no basis in reality.

The fact is, however, that this statement is far from religious jargon. In its earliest conception, it referred to the very real world and experience of the people being addressed, many of whom relied on farming acumen for their survival. It meant then, as it does now, that the care, precision and attention given to the planting and nurturing of the seeds one planted, would determine in large measure the quality and quantity of the harvest one reaped.

The great teachers of ancient times used this statement as an analogy because all could relate to it. The purpose was to point out, that just as the success of the harvest was directly related to the care and attention given to the seed, so it was in all areas of life, including health, prosperity, happiness and the quality of personal relationships.

They were trying to use a simple concept that everyone could grasp, to convey the basic nature of life. It is as practical as it is profound. It is also one of the basic tenets that are common to many of the world's great philosophies. However, while it is as relevant today as it has ever been, it is also, as difficult to hear. Regardless, there is no doubt about the fundamental truth behind the statement.

In order to find a substitute for those forbidding and archaic sounding words, *sow* and *reap*, our current culture has come up with its own version. It is, *What Goes Around, Comes Around,* and is generally accepted as a basic "truism." Because it has no whiff of religiosity, even though it means exactly the same thing as, *as you sow, so shall you reap*, we can more readily *hear* it. In addition, somewhere deep down inside, we mostly accept the meaning behind it, namely that:

*What you are getting out of life is a direct result of what you are putting in.*

Imagine what life would be like if the people you live, work and interact with, all suddenly became convinced that every single thought, word and action that emerged from them actually counted? That these things did not just disappear into the air like smoke, but rather formed the very fabric that would become their future life's experience. In other words, that *what goes around, does indeed, come around!*

What if this understanding of their causative power awoke them to their own ability to improve or destroy the quality of their own lives to such a degree that they all started being their best possible selves at all times? More to the point, what would *your* life be like if just you were suddenly the best possible person that you could be?

Most everyone would like to be a better person and live a higher quality, more fulfilling life. The question has always been, *how?* How does one deal with all the pressures and challenges that life constantly presents to block an individual from always doing and being their best? What is the answer?

Many think that the only place to find that kind of wisdom is in the great works of the past. Arguments rage over the interpretive significance and the historical accuracy and relevance of such works as the old and new Testaments, the Quran, the Upanishads, the Zohar, and the canons of eastern and western philosophies. Academics can spend their entire working lives on a quest for clues and archeological verification to support their views.

This reflects a belief that two or three thousand years ago humanity had greater access to truth and understanding than is the case today, when the fact is that truth is both as elusive and as accessible today as it has been at any time in history. In addition, just as in all previous times, a large portion of it remains behind the closed doors of human potential, not locked away, but awaiting for the opening of the door to be revealed.

It is curious to ponder why the human race is on such a treadmill when it comes to wisdom. It can take years of experience to acquire what seems like a thimble-full of insight and each generation appears to require going through it all over again. While there has arguably been a steady ebb of progress over the world as a whole, it is a rare parent who does not bemoan how difficult it is to impart their hard-earned knowledge to their own children in an effort to save them from unnecessary hardship.

It seems as if each succeeding generation needs to have their own experiences and go through their own ups and downs in order for anything to sink in. When all is said and done, each must discover their truth for themselves.

We are in the early stages now, however, of an interesting period and the dichotomy could not be greater. While in some parts of the world individual freedoms are being crushed, in others there is a greater emphasis being placed on self-discovery than at any previous point in history. In the latter, change has been so pervasive and swift that many of our frontiers have all but vanished. As Eric Butterworth put it:

> *"Today the last remaining frontier is in the realm of the inner person. In the face of the awesome challenges confronting mankind, there is nowhere to go but in."*

Of course, the hope of anyone reading this is that we find our collective way to planetary, peaceful co-existence. How and if that ultimately gets achieved is a continuous work in progress, just as we all are individually.

The next great step of the race is the quest to learn how each is connected to the whole, and uncovering the mystery of, *how life really works.* The purpose of this book is to facilitate that adventure, assisting each reader in shaping a happier, healthier, more prosperous and rewarding life.

# A Story About Clayton

*I first met Clayton when I went to work for an investment banking firm where he was a senior partner. Responsible for managing a major department of the firm he was constantly sought out for one-on-one meetings by clients who wanted to plumb his views on world markets. To say he was in demand and busy is an understatement of significant proportion.*

*During my tenure with this firm, I had many opportunities to observe him in these client meetings during which he was uniformly impressive. These all paled, however, in comparison to another quite different interaction I had with Clayton.*

*It was quite customary in this firm for different departments to engage in friendly athletic competition. So it was that we gathered one Sunday afternoon on the field of a lovely, suburban school to get to know each other better through a camaraderie-building game of soccer.*

*I had played some soccer in college and felt fairly confident that I wouldn't embarrass myself. I arrived early, stretched and jogged around the field to prepare myself.*

*The other combatants ranged from just out of college, to the 30's crowd where I resided, to a group in their 50's, including Clayton. In short order, teams were organized and play began.*

*I have several impressions of the game but mostly I remember Clayton out-hustling me and others to a loose ball over and over again – coming out of nowhere to take the ball away as I was about to shoot at the goal – stealing a pass and racing downfield to score a goal himself.*

*It was a close game won by a single goal, score: 8 to 7 (the winner shall remain a mystery). At the end, just about everyone lay sprawled in the grass exhausted from the intensity of the game. Everyone, that is, except Clayton. There he was, the oldest one on the field, bustling about handing* out cans of soda and patting everyone on the back. "Good game, good game," he could be heard saying over and over.

I don't know if he noticed me that day, but I sure noticed him. "Wow, " I thought, "Here's the oldest guy on the field and he's a dynamo. He's all over the place. How does he do it?" I resolved that I would find out. Not long after, I had an opportunity.

Later that week I had to see someone in Clayton's department. When I was finished, I gathered my nerve and marched to his office to see him. I'd just ask him directly, I figured. Well, he wasn't in having just left, his very official secretary informed me. I must have looked very disappointed because she asked me what the problem was and whether she could help.

I was very hesitant and a bit embarrassed to explain that I wanted to ask Clayton, the senior partner of the firm, how in heck he could be in such great shape at his age, but something in her manner encouraged me. I blurted out the whole story of the game and how I was compelled to find out more about this man.

She smiled and told me to sit down. "You know," she said, "He's a very private and shy person. If you asked him directly, I doubt that he would even be able to answer since the truth might sound a bit like bragging, which he'd never do. I will fill you in, though, if you promise to keep it a secret just between us." I did and have, until now. To compromise, I have changed his name in this story and hope that I'm still being sufficiently true to the spirit of that word. If not, I know I'll pay for it.

Clayton, she explained, was a man who believed in a balanced life. He worked hard, was devoted to his family, attended church regularly and actively participated in athletics. He believed that each activity one engaged in should be done with total concentration and focus.

Clayton's view was that an individual's responsibilities included doing their job as best they could, taking care of their family and keeping them-selves in good physical, emotional, and spiritual shape. He believed that without a strong physical body to support the individual, that career and family would surely suffer. As a result, he exercised vigorously every day.

*"Every day," I retorted. "How could a guy with so many demands exercise every day? I could sit at my desk 28 hours a day and still not feel that my work was done. His job is ten times more complex than mine. How does he do it?" She smiled again.*

*"See this," she said, pointing to his appointment book. "If he doesn't have an official luncheon appointment, he goes to the gym and works out. He never has lunch for fun. If he does have a lunch date, he automatically has a vital, out-of-the-office meeting at 10:30 where he is unreachable (at the gym, of course). He very rarely gives up both time slots on any given day." By maintaining that discipline, she explained, Clayton was able to maintain a high level of physical conditioning and do it in the context of his day. That was important, she said, because he liked to reserve evenings for his wife and children. She pointed out that his resolve at maintaining this discipline had not seemed to hurt his professional stature.*

On the contrary, Clayton believed that staying strong physically allowed him to work harder, handle pressure more easily, stay focused and be generally more effective in everything he did. It also gave him the energy to be present for his wife and kids when he got home. It was all part of the balance. Clayton had a clear idea of what he wanted to achieve. His actions supported that idea fully and the results were exemplary.

Although he will never know the profound effect he had on me, there were many occasions over the years, when I was feeling too tired, lazy, busy, pressured or whatever to stick with my exercise program, when I have thought of that conversation. "If a guy with as much going on and as much responsibility as Clayton can exercise regularly," I reasoned, "then I'm an irresponsible, wimp to do otherwise." Thankfully, it's usually worked.

# A Thought: *Principles of Life*

*Living*
*an*
*Effective, Dynamic*
*and*
*Successful Life*

*Requires*
*Understanding and Complying*
*With the*
*Principles*

*Which*
*Determine*
*Life's*
*Course.*

# The Law of Cause and Effect

Most people come to realize at some point, that getting along in life involves adhering to certain ground rules or guidelines. These may be written or not, actual laws of society or generally understood, but unwritten laws of nature:

> *The time it takes to understand, accept and learn*
> *to live in harmony with these laws has a lot to*
> *do with the quality of a person's life.*

Obviously, Clayton had been well-schooled in such principles through his family, education, friends, and his own efforts, and was comfortable living his life with them in mind. Life cooperated with him, as a result. JRT, on the other hand, is more reminiscent of a certain kind of child one can remember from their school days.

He was the kid who had difficulty dealing effectively with guidelines. As a result, he had to deal with the consequences. As years go by, most people figure it out and adjust. Others such as JRT never do, and go through life in a constant struggle. They cause disharmony and turmoil for themselves and those around them.

Hopefully though, most people do make progress and continue to learn – stubbing a toe here and there or burning a finger occasionally – to develop the awareness that in nature, *there are various laws that determine how different aspects of life work.* These laws are not religious, philosophical nor esoteric, but rather scientific. They are exact, specific and unswerving. Many of these laws and the principles they illuminate have been discovered, or rather uncovered by humankind, which has enabled humans to work in harmony with them and achieve previously unimagined results.

The way electricity has been harnessed and utilized in all sorts of ways beneficial to humankind is an example. Nobody invented electricity. On the contrary, the principles of the *Law of Electricity* existed long before Nikola Tesla and Thomas Edison stumbled across them. Once they did, however, and came to understand the power of those principles, they figured out ways to work in harmony with them to produce great good in the world.

*They knew that while we cannot change nature, we can through intelligent choice, improve our relationship with it.*

Likewise, nobody invented planting and cultivating a tulip bulb so that it grows into a beautiful flower. Somewhere along the line people discovered which actions produced great looking tulips. Those steps were then recorded and practiced over and over to produce striking blossoms.

The gardener learns that if certain steps are followed carefully and weather conditions cooperate, the chances are pretty good that a healthy flower will grow. It is hard to conceive that a gardener who understands the principles involved would plant the bulb and then not provide sufficient water, light or some other necessary conditions, thereby assuring that flower's early demise.

The same can be said for a chef's careful preparation of a valued recipe. The formula was arrived at no doubt, after countless attempts to find just the right temperature, blend of ingredients, and time in the oven. It represents the best understanding the chef has to date of which steps to follow in order to accomplish the goal, namely a delicious meal. A savvy student then follows these steps intelligently and meticulously.

The chef may, of course, freely use his intelligence to refine his understanding. It is difficult to imagine, however, that he would drastically change some elements of the recipe and still expect the same result achieved in the past.

*Each case shows the discovery or uncovering of law, and the intelligent utilization of that law to achieve some desired results.*

Every child begins to learn about these Laws at an early point in life. Heat water to a certain temperature and it will boil every time. Put an egg into that water for a certain number of minutes and it will become hard-boiled, every time.

It is the understanding and intelligent application of such Laws as these that allowed Thomas Edison, Henry Ford, George Washington Carver, Alexander Graham Bell, the Wright brothers and all the others to make their significant contributions.

Eventually, we all come to know, to a greater or lesser degree, that there are certain rules involved in everything we do. We know that if we want to achieve a certain goal, there are certain steps we must follow, and further, that if we follow those steps more closely and with a greater sense of purpose, we will accomplish our goal with even greater certainty.

This understanding has been proven literally millions of times. In fact, every aspect of nature and life operates according to the *principles* of the *law* involved.

For example:

*The repetition of precise steps to prepare lawns and gardens for each season in order to achieve the desired effect.*

*The careful preparation of a favorite recipe attempting to capture the exact measure of ingredients, temperature, and timing that was so successful previously.*

*The never-ending quest of every golfer and tennis player to recapture the precise set of movements and coordination of the parts that produced that great shot.*

In all these cases, an awareness exists, that a certain set of circumstances presented under certain conditions, will always produce a particular result, and that correspondingly, every result can be traced to a particular cause. Stated in another way:

*FOR EVERY CONDITION OR EFFECT THAT EXISTS
IN LIFE THERE IS A CORRESPONDING CAUSE*

*AND*

*EVERY ACTION OR CAUSE IN LIFE GENERATES A
CORRESPONDING EFFECT OR CONDITION*

This concept has been expressed in many ways, but is referred to here as:

*THE LAW OF CAUSE AND EFFECT*

This is the basic Law of Life, underlying all laws of nature and human experience.

| *Quality of Thoughts, Words and Actions* | *Quality of Life* |
|:---:|:---:|
| CAUSE | EFFECT |

*This formula applies in equal measure in every individual's life regardless of family stature, career, wealth, race, religion, or any other measure.*

It has been demonstrated that this law applies equally to positive and negative input. The law itself just follows the lead provided by each individual, to produce in kind, what is presented. The individual alone is the ultimate arbiter, or selector of the input which the law is compelled to respond to. These stories about people I have known illustrate this law in action.

# A Thought: *Watch What's Held As Truth*

*In this world*
*One's dominion*
*Over their own life*

*Is determined solely*
*By their knowledge, beliefs*
*And willingness to change*

*Yet grasping this fact*
*And putting it in practice*
*Is only the first step*

*Continual watchfulness*
*For the duration*
*Then becomes*
*The quest*

*As an ancient sage once said...*

*The price of liberty*
*Is eternal vigilance*

*for...*

*According to your belief*
*It is done unto you*

# A Story About Herbert

*Herb was a mostly fun and fascinating study in contrasts. He was an important friend and mentor to me at a time in life when I needed guidance, something he gave with humor and gusto. Unfortunately, he passed away long before his time from his particular demon, smoking-induced emphysema.*

*Herb was bright, witty, good-natured and almost always a pleasure to be around. Naturally, he was adored by his family and a wide circle of friends. He also achieved a certain level of success, and while the preservation of money was not one of his strong points, he always seemed to live well and enjoy life. That is until his habitual smoking began to wreak havoc on his physical body.*

*I knew Herb as well as anyone. Despite our age difference, we were close friends and business associates. The tale of how that came to be is a story unto itself, but one we'll save that for another day. Without question, Herb was the most charming conversationalist, quickest quipper and most potent punster I've ever seen in action. To say it again – it was very hard not to like Herbert.*

*Herb's life was a veritable whirlwind of events. He was a fountain of ideas for new ventures, or ways to improve existing ones. When he focused his tremendous energy on some challenge, you could be sure that positive change would follow quickly and detractors would soon be converted to fans.*

*This was a function of what I described as Herb's unassailable good nature. He only would advocate actions which were clearly for the greater good of all involved and he considered it fundamental to leave no stone unturned in his quest to find a solution that would achieve it. It did not take long for people to figure out that Herb really didn't have it in for them, but rather was sincerely interested in their success.*

The result, not too surprisingly, was that Herb's ideas were usually embraced so enthusiastically by the participants that they literally could not fail. Whether or not his proposal was the best possible one for the situation was less of a factor than the wholehearted enthusiasm he was able to generate.

Herb, on his level and in his own way, did a lot of good and affected a great many people in a positive way, including me. In a manner of speaking, Herbert had a certain brilliance, and I was fortunate enough to experience a good dose of it firsthand.

"How, How, How!" they wailed. "Why, Why, Why!" they cried. It began when he was first admitted, choking, coughing and spitting, to the hospital. The doctors said his lungs were full of gunk and unless he stopped smoking, he would die. He stayed in the hospital for about two weeks that first time. About two minutes after he left, he lit up.

In his close, personal world, Herbert had two grown children, a brother, an ex-wife and three current or former girlfriends, all of whom he stayed in touch and was friends with. In addition, he had many friends he'd known anywhere from 40 years to 2 days who swore admiration, adulation and affection in varying degrees, including me.

How could a guy who was so terrific, who obviously got so much joy from life and who had so many people who adored him, be so self-destructive as to smoke after such a near disaster?

Well, that near disaster turned into another, then another, then another. On a visit during one of these episodes, I was fixing Herb's pillow so he could sit up when I discovered a cigarette under the pillow. He was near death, breathing through a mask connected to an oxygen tank, and he had talked one of the nurses into giving him a cigarette, such were his powers. He almost expired on the spot from rage when I tossed it out of the window before his eyes.

Then one day, I received a call from his current lady informing me tearfully of the end ... and of the plans for his memorial service. How unbelievable, I thought. One of the greatest individuals I've ever known kills *himself because in one particular area, he was so out of control and made such bad choices.*

*It taught me that a person can be terrific in certain aspects of life, but awful in others. That greatness in some area, doesn't mean the whole person is great. It taught me that even in the same life, there can be evidence of positive choices right alongside proof of poor ones.*

*Herb was a fitting example of a dichotomy that exists in everyone to some extent. He was also a great friend and a stellar role model for me in many ways. I really miss you, Herb.*

...and then there was Louise...

# A Story About Louise

*Louise, oh Louise, I still don't get it. I don't think I ever will. You were a good friend. I cared about you. Many did. You were brilliant, attractive, charming, funny, successful...what gives? What was missing? How is it to be explained? It is surely not understandable. Oh Louise, I missed you for a long time. I thought about you a lot. Eventually, I stopped. I had to. But every now and then you pop back into my brain...*

I met Louise through my friend Jerry. They had grown up together in a small town outside of Albany. Both had ended up in New York City with successful careers. They were ranked one and two academically in their high school graduating class, though neither would reveal who was which. Such was their mutual though platonic affection.

One spring, Jerry called to ask if I might be interested in joining him and several of his friends who were renting a summer house on Fire Island. They had one share left and he was sure that I would enjoy the group. The house, he explained, was in a fairly private community, sparsely populated by couples and families.

Its privacy derived from the fact that it required a lengthy hike along the shore from where the ferry docked to get there. No paths or walkways had yet been installed. Jerry in his usual fashion, put the most positive spin on what could be taken as either "the good news" or "the bad news." I said, "Great, count me in."

When the first weekend arrived, I met the group at the ferry in Bayshore on Long Island. Optimistic anticipation of a good time abounded. There were six people sharing the house that weekend and Jerry was the only one I knew. The third guy was a market research exec named Barry. His girlfriend Marty, an older gal he worked with named Sylvia, and Jerry's friend, Louise rounded out the group. Like Jerry, Louise was in the advertising business. She was a senior account executive with a major agency and had just completed her master's degree in marketing.

The ride across the Great South Bay was pure delight. As the shore of Long Island faded into the distance, whatever tension I'd been feeling just faded along with it. The sky was blue with a few clouds overhead and the banter pleasant. Jerry introduced me to everyone and within moments, I fell into easy conversation with the group. Before long, the shore of Fire Island came into view. As we approached, the group grew quiet in anticipation of our arrival.

Only Jerry and Louise had actually seen the house which they had alternately described as fabulous, charming, warm, etc. All we knew for sure was that it was a serious hike from the ferry. Due to the fact that it was our first weekend, the house had no provisions, meaning that, in addition to our clothes we also had a load of food items which had to be transported. Normally, people used wagons pulled along the path or boardwalk for such chores. In our case, it was strictly people power.

"No sweat," said Jerry. We'll just take our time and be there before we know it. "That's why I invited Rob," he said. "Strong like bull."

"You mean mule," I replied.

Well, so much for best laid plans, etc. Within minutes of disembarking and starting our trek, the skies began to darken ominously. What followed was not your gentle summer shower kind of rain. It was, rather, a torrential downpour complete with thunder and flashes of lightning. Here we were, walking along the edge of the shore loaded down with duffels and bags of food. Wind and rain whipped at us from what seemed like all sides at once.

"My God, what do we do?" someone gasped. Though I was the stranger in the group, action was required and I took charge. I looked around and quickly spotted a likely looking pile of rocks. "Okay everyone, bring the food over here before the bags break." I took the packages and placed them in the crags of the rocks where I hoped they would survive until I could retrieve them.

"Now let's head for the house."

Lightened up, we were able to pick up the pace. I grabbed Sylvia's bag so she could keep up. Barry did the same for Marty. When Jerry laughingly offered to carry Louise's bag, she suggested that we'd probably get there faster if she carried Jerry's instead. It was a welcome bit of levity that lifted everyone's spirit a bit. When Jerry shouted out, "There it is," we were probably the happiest and most relieved group of six people on the planet at that moment. We were also in varying degrees of utter soaked exhaustion, but thankfully at least, we were there.

The place was indeed terrific, but enjoying it would have to wait. The light was fading outside and every bit of food we had was back on the rocks. I figured that since I was already soaked, there was no time like the present. A quick appraisal of the group led me to conclude that I was the only one in the bunch capable of making the trip. I dumped the clothes out of my bag so I could use it for the food and headed out the door.

I moved quickly with the empty bag and had made some progress when I heard the shout, "Hey, wait for me." It was Louise. She'd grabbed a cloth shopping bag from the kitchen and followed. She had really moved to catch me. We found the stash moments later and were able to repack everything we'd left behind. It really helped having an extra pair of hands. Louise was terrific. The rain letup a bit and we walked back in high spirits. By the time we burst through the door to the cheers of our companions, we were buddies.

Needless to say, I was treated to a great dinner that night. Everyone in the group except me was skilled in the kitchen. In the future, I would wash a lot of dishes, but on this night, I was relieved of all duties. Following a well-deserved hot shower, Louise on the other hand, jumped right in and prepared a fabulous salad. I was more than content to watch, glass of wine in hand.

The summer was great, as was the next – same group – same house. We took lots of long walks on the beach, swam in the ocean, had fierce battles of bridge, ate unbelievable meals on very clean dishes and got to know each other well. Louise and I had these stop and go romantic interludes, but *they didn't last. She'd get distracted and disappear. She liked to be around me, but not too close. It was confusing but eventually I just accepted it. Once the summer ended so did the interludes, but not the friendship.*

*Jerry's call blew my mind.*

*"Rob, I need you to go to the hospital with me. A cleaning man found Louise hanging from the window of her office on the 35th floor, by her fingers. He pulled her in, but they took her to the hospital for observation. I'm afraid to go by myself. Will you come?"*

*"What happened?" Jerry asked her.*

*"I don't know," she said. "I'm not happy. I'm scared I never will be. Why live?"*

*We stayed a long time. We talked and talked, though I was in shock the whole time. "Louise," I wanted to say. "You're such a terrific person. I would be with you and try to make you happy, but you won't let me in."*

*I didn't say it though. I'd tried it before, back when. It hadn't worked. I felt bad, really helpless. Eventually they made us leave so Louise could sleep. She went to Albany for a couple of weeks with her parents. Then she was back as though nothing had happened.*

*I saw Louise a couple of times that spring. We'd talk about what was happening in life, but stayed away from the window incident. But to some degree however, it was always present, like a cloud over the proceedings. Jerry's next call, while all the more devastating, was also in a way less of a surprise.*

*Louise lived on the top floor of a six-story brownstone in the West Village. She had jumped off her terrace and landed on the concrete below. Contrary to her intentions, however, she lived. A neighbor sitting outside on his terrace had seen her flash by and immediately called for emergency help. Though she had broken bones and ruptured organs, she was in the hospital and it looked like she would survive.*

*It is difficult to describe what it was like to see her that day. Only in the movies do you see scenes like that, but there she was. Her comment from the last incident flashed through my mind. "I'm not happy. I'm scared I never will be. Why live?" Okay, I thought, I get down. Everyone does. But come on. You've so much going for you. Why this? But there was nothing I could say. On this day, she couldn't hear me if I tried. Her breathing was all there was. Jerry wept.*

*When she was released, she went to her parents' again. This time her recovery took about nine months. Once, I made the drive with Jerry to see her. We walked and talked about stuff. She brought up our adventure in the rain. Talking about it cheered her up and we laughed at the thought of the bedraggled, sopping bunch we were that day.*

*She never made it back to her life in the city. There were some hopeful signs, and even a party planned for what we thought was another try. However, a near miss, this time with a gun, short-circuited that idea. Eventually she succeeded. Jerry called to tell me. He was disconsolate. She had shut herself in her car, in her parents' garage with the engine on. Her mom had found her.*

When I think about Louise I ask myself, and others have posed the same question, "Did Louise even have a choice?" Admittedly, it's way over my head to understand that kind of pain. Some would say that neither Louise nor Herb are actually appropriate illustrations for this book because for them there was no choice. It is a particularly sensitive matter for those who have experienced similar trauma with a close friend or family. I feel them.

But, when I think hard on it, nobody helped Herb to light up, and likewise as tragic as it is, Sylvia planned out each step carefully. She alone closed the garage doors, and she alone put the key in that ignition and turned it on. She would still be with us, except that she so didn't want to be.

So ultimately I have to conclude that yes, she was the one who did make those choices, the last one of which finally worked! Honestly however, if you feel you have reason to disagree, you have every right. Because you know why? It's another one of those things in life, the *truth* of which is simply unknowable. In the end, the best we can hope to draw from such stark examples, is some lesson for ourselves about the ramifications of the decisions that *we* make each moment of every day.

# THE CHALLENGE

From a practical standpoint, it is appropriate to acknowledge that in the real world as we experience it, no individual's *quality of thoughts, words, and actions (cause)* are either all great or all terrible, just as the *quality of life experience (effect)* is never completely perfect or horrible. There is, in every life, a constant flowing mix. The challenge is to improve on the mix.

Think of it like a scale from 1-10, 1 representing the worst/lowest quality and 10 the highest. Furthermore, there is a scale to measure every aspect of one's life. One may do really well on two or three spectrums but not so well on others. Stories abound about athletes, politicians, clergy, business people, artists and others who make this point – world class at some things – dismal at others. The relevant question is: Where am I – where are you on those scales of 1-10, and how can we individually and collectively move higher?

To do so, it helps for each individual to realize and come to grips with the implications of the following:

- There is a direct and inexorable linkage between the two sides of the equation. (Reference the scale on page 79)
- When the *cause* side of the equation (quality of thoughts, words and actions) is altered either positively or negatively, that alteration is exactly reflected in the *effect* side of the equation (the quality of one's life experience).

If what has been described resonates and one accepts this linkage of cause and effect as the truth for themselves, then it follows that they must also view the understanding of *how life really works* as a matter of the great consequence. That individual's most important ongoing challenge is then, to think, speak and act accordingly, even as life presents the constant pressures to do otherwise. Chip, who you met earlier, plus Caitlin who's up next provide eloquent examples on the subject.

Chip is an example of people who purposefully change the *cause* side of their equation when they decide they are not pleased with the *effect* they are creating in their lives. In her own unique way, Caitlin does the same.

It seems apparent, that while people may be aware of the *Law of Cause and Effect* in the outer world of nature, they generally lack the comprehension that *it is just as active in their own individual lives as it is in any other part of life.*

It is easy to comprehend that planting a healthy tulip bulb under proper care and conditions will result in the growth of a beautiful flower called a tulip, and equally obvious to acknowledge that if left unattended, the tulip may never grow or may be strangled by weeds. These are both examples of the *Law of Cause and Effect* at work.

It is a tremendous leap of understanding, though, for most individuals, no matter how educated or sophisticated, to see the quality of their own life as the direct *effect* of their own input or *cause,* as clearly as if they were planting seeds and tending the garden.

Returning to the tulip, when cared for properly, the result was positive. When not cared for properly, it was negative. The only difference was how *the law* was used. It really made no difference to *the law* what the gardener did – *the law* did not render judgment and call the gardener either good or bad – *the law* just reacted to the input, or *cause* by producing the appropriate result or *effect.*

*The Law of Cause and Effect is a neutral force. It does not interpret. Rather, it responds according to the input it receives. If the input is negative, it punishes. If the input is positive, it rewards. The Law is straightforward and treats all even-handedly. It has been written that, the law is no respecter of persons and will bring good or evil to any, according to their use or misuse of it.*

Is there a deity watching the proceedings and rendering both judgement and punishment? For those who would like that to be the case so they could place the blame there rather than in the mirror, sorry. There is no such genie. Just your choices. Can I offer a coherent explanation for why this is the case? Nope! It's one of those things I mentioned that are not explainable. But is it true? Well... does it resonate as true to you? Because that is all that matters. If it does, read on! If not, sorry no refunds.

> *Life responds to each person by producing results*
> *that correspond exactly with their input.*

It is as exact and precise as the law of electricity, gravity, aerodynamics, or any other law of life and nature. The paradox is that while it is so obvious in so many ways, most people seem to have a blind spot when it comes to understanding and accepting the function of this law in the workings of their own life. Consider the following:

1) Student A - Is aware that there is a spelling test each Friday, studies a sufficient amount each night leading up to the test and arrives at school on Friday prepared for the test.

*- versus -*

Student B - Is also aware of the Friday spelling test, reads magazines and listens to music each night, when not out with friends, only glancing at the words briefly before school on Friday.

2) Father A - Professes to love his three children and endeavors to spend time with them collectively as well as individually. He makes a point to be home at least one night each week for a family dinner and plans at least one family activity each weekend. He makes sure he is available for special school functions for parents.

*- versus -*

Father B - Professes to love his three children and vows to spend more time with them in the future than he has in the past. He finds it necessary, though, to work late most nights. Weekends find him mainly on the tennis courts or golf course, which he considers a priority due to his need for relaxation. He can never seem to make the school functions due to crucial meetings that come up.

3) Worker A - Is always at work on time with a positive attitude. He arrives ready for action with the necessary preparations completed. He spends the day focused on his duties, which he treats and speaks of respectfully, since they are the vehicle by which he supports his family and life. He treats his co-workers and superiors professionally and respectfully.

*- versus -*

Worker B - Is frequently late for work and constantly pushes against the constraints of appropriate behavior. Although talented, he is never quite prepared. He often wastes much of the day for himself and others by chatting about unrelated matters and gossiping. He rarely misses an opportunity to speak badly about a colleague or supervisor.

These are of patterns of human behavior we have all observed in ourselves or others. In fact, I have personally known all but one of the individuals described herein. Perhaps you have as well. One should have little difficulty imagining the quality of life they will experience as a result of their choices.

These examples are presented to illustrate that every individual does in fact, have a direct input – the choices they make *(cause)*, into what will emerge as the quality of their life experience *(effect)*.

The extent to which an individual can grasp this concept and then exercise purposeful control over the *cause* aspect of the *law of cause and effect,* will directly and exactly impact the *effect* side, which is the quality of that individual's life experience.

However, let me be the first to say that exercising *purposeful control* is no simple matter. First, one must understand why they should even try.  Grasping the precision and pervasive working of the *Law of Cause and Effect* in all areas of one's life is a good first step.  Consider....

*"Take away all the trappings,*
*the sophistication, the cultivated games,*
*the mastered technique,*
*the station in life one inherits or achieves,*
*and all are left with one basic quality,*

CHOICE.

*Whether industrialist, professor,*
*mason, painter or priest,*
*all individuals,*
*each on their own level of life,*
*choose how they think about,*
*speak to, and act toward,*
*people and conditions in their lives ...."*

*The*
*LAW OF CAUSE AND EFFECT*
*serves as a guide*
*for making these choices.*

# A Thought: *Seeds To Plant*

*I basked in the love of my child tonight*

*She asked if I'd play some cards and I said sure*

*While we played we listened to some music she likes*

*And spoke of matters of life she was curious about*

*She ended up curled in my lap tired and ready for bed*

*I had the privilege of tucking her in*

*I got a wonderful hug and kiss on the cheek*

*There are times when I've said I'm too busy*

*When that's happened all I can think of is*

*I must have lost my mind*

# A Story About Caitlin

*There is absolutely no truth to the rampant conjecture that the reason I consider Caitlin to be a knockout combo of great personality, brilliant mind plus beauty inside and out, is that I had the privilege of helping to raise her. In fact, from the moment I met her, along with sister Vanessa and twin brother Courtney, all of those qualities were readily apparent. Not that there haven't been challenges along the way to her full realization of those qualities. In fact, I have had many opportunities to question what may have become of them. Naturally, through them all I consistently handled everything perfectly, never once losing my perspective, patience, temper or sense of humor... sure.*

*There is one incident about Caitlin's high school experience that stands out in my mind. She had attended a private girls' school, call it the Academy, for pretty much the duration, and consistently succeeded academically. When eighth grade rolled around, however, she began agitating in favor of going to the public high school. Her rationale was that she felt she should experience a more well-rounded environment. In other words, she wanted to be around boys.*

*The matter was discussed at length, experts were consulted. In the end, we decided to let Caitlin make the call herself though her mother and I both had mixed feelings. Neither of us were sure what that right thing to do really was. She had been such a good student and a good kid that we decided to go with her preference.*

*It was some time before there was any discernible difference in either Caitlin's behavior or her performance. Slowly, however, things started to shift. The "Academy" had prioritized issues such as self-discipline, punctuality, dress code, language, maintaining good study habits and high academic standards. The high school, on the other hand, being quite large and diverse, pretty much left those matters up to each individual to figure out for themselves.*

*Some students thrived in that atmosphere, excelling and going on to terrific colleges and universities. Others floundered. There is no question that the resources were there. It was left up to the student, though, to take advantage of them.*

*This is not to suggest that Caitlin fell off the cliff. Rather, A's became B's and so forth. Her dress habits, however, shifted fairly quickly toward every father's nightmare, along with her attitude, which took on a more surly quality. Still ninth grade ended on a reasonably high note. Her ingrained study habits supported her at finals time, and she was able to pull off grades at her usual level.*

*Tenth grade was another story. It started rough and stayed that way. Her grades slipped and there were episodes that made us wonder if we'd made a horrible mistake by letting her change schools. It seemed like we were losing the terrific girl we loved so much and it scared us. Of course, this is the common lament of most parents of teenagers, but even knowing that to be the case was of little comfort at the time.*

*The answer to what to do, actually came from Caitlin herself. One evening after a particularly difficult confrontation about what was happening, she asked to speak with us. She revealed that she felt as if she had, in fact, lost herself. She said that her confidence and self-control had disappeared. The anger and frustration she'd been expressing to us had as much to do with her disappointment with herself as with our parental controls. Not, she was compelled to throw in that those controls were needed. She was, after all, a woman of almost sixteen years old!*

*In one of the more lucid moments of self-examination I've experienced with anyone, Caitlin told us she was concerned that she might not be able to "pull it together" on command anymore and that her hopes of getting into a good college were sliding into the sunset. Since she had made such a big deal about leaving the Academy to go to the high school in the first place, she'd been scared and embarrassed, she explained, to reveal her concerns.*

*Was there any way, she wondered, that we would consider letting her return to the Academy, if they'd accept her back for her final two years? Needless to say, we again supported her decision.*

*The Academy gladly accepted Caitlin back for her junior year. Her approach to her academics returned overnight and her grades reflected it. Other issues of teenage-hood remained as serious parental challenges, but we were thrilled to have her voluntarily back in the environment that supported and brought forth her best.*

*The result of Caitlin's decision to take charge of the direction in which she was heading, had several ramifications. She put herself back into an environment where there was positive reinforcement for doing the things necessary for her to achieve academic excellence. This included proper rest and diet as well as correct study skills.*

Seeing Caitlin now as a grown woman and terrific mother with four girls and one boy, is a joy. And, as this is written, three of those girls are at the Academy in their respective grades. Who knows where she'd be if our discussions took a different path. But it is clear that her choice to come clean and change direction was big.

# THE STAKE

Some people consider attention to the issues we've been discussing to be a matter of convenience rather than necessity. They feel that as long as everything is going just fine – and particularly if *someone* else is paying attention – then acting with the *Law of Cause and Effect* in mind is a good idea. If, however, there is a problem or conflict at hand, or the opportunity to take advantage of a particular situation, especially if *nobody* appears to be in a position to notice – then the concern is often dismissed as unnecessary.

It is, in fact, quite easy to understand why this is the case. If one sees no particular connection between what they think, say and do (as long as they don't get caught) and conditions that life will subsequently present them with, then why be concerned?

*It is only by grasping the very real consequences that one can develop the interest and motivation to understand the mechanics of how the Law of Cause and Effect works, and thereby take control of life rather than remain an apparent victim, at the mercy of what appears to be either good or bad luck.*

The truth is that one either creates the conditions they want through knowledge and correct application or they create conditions that seem like bad luck through ignorance and denial of their right, responsibility and ability to choose intelligently. In each case, the individual creates their own experience. The difference is that the former knows it while the latter does not.

There are cases, when a person's realization of the impact their choices make, can assist that person in waking up to what they are thinking, saying and doing. It is very often, however, not until the aftermath of one's behavior has unfolded that one sees clearly the power they exert in their own particular world.

Consider the following categories and personalize them in your own life. Think of what each means to you and what your impact truly is. Many do not give enough thought to the consequences a particular action might cause in those parts of their life that mean the most. It's only afterward that they may say:

*How could I have done that to my spouse – Gee, I never thought about how that would affect my child – If I could only take that word or action back.*

Everyone slips from time to time because we are all human. But many of the slips could be avoided, if we operated as often as possible, mindful of the Law of Cause and Effect. Consider ....

*YOUR HOME – YOUR FAMILY – YOUR CAREER*

*YOUR LIFE*

*THESE ARE AT STAKE*

# A Story About Mildred

*Mildred was my mother. She died from lung cancer, the result of years of at least one pack a day of Chesterfield cigarettes. She had stopped the smoking some years before but the disease had apparently already taken root by then.*

*Not that she wasn't ready to go. She often decried what she found to be an unfulfilling existence without the presence of her beloved husband of more than forty years. He had been gone for several, also the victim of cancer. In his case, it was brought about, I am convinced, by his prolific pipe smoking. It may have had its charm, but it was ultimately deadly. He was gone way before it was necessary or natural.*

*They were, in their ways, a great couple. Sure, they went through their wars with each other, but they hung in, raised three children and loved each other like crazy. After he was gone and my mother moved, first closer to me and then nearer to my sister, his presence was always palpable in the apartments she occupied.*

*I'd walk in and say, "Hi Dad."*

*She'd say, "I feel him too. He's always here."*

*We'd laugh. "Just can't escape him, huh," I'd joke.*

*"Don't want to. Never did. Miss him so," she'd sigh.*

*"Okay, okay, enough of that," I'd recover. "I'm here now. Let's play cards!"*

*She'd smile, "Yes darling, I'm so glad you're here. What game?"*

*One of the many things that impressed me about my mother was the way she pulled together their financial situation late in their lives. They had always lived with a fairly cavalier attitude about finances, rooted in their very strong belief that life would always provide them with what they needed. In fact, even though my father's income was very erratic, it seemed to do just that. Until, that is, the "shock" occurred.*

*My dad seemed like a bull of a man. He worked hard, had a voracious appetite for literature and was an avid cook and gardener. He projected the powerful sense of a person who created his own world and would go on doing so forever. Then he got sick. He was struck by an infection that was related to a childhood bout with rheumatic fever. It had almost killed him then, and did in fact take his younger brother, my Uncle Edward.*

*My father detested being in any hospital and went to great lengths to avoid ever seeing doctors. This, no doubt, contributed mightily to causing his condition to deteriorate as it did, to the point where he literally collapsed at home and was rushed by ambulance to the hospital. He was in such bad shape that he needed massive doses of antibiotics administered intravenously for a period of six weeks.*

*Much to his chagrin, he was forced to remain hospitalized for that entire period. Thankfully, while undergoing tests, his doctors discovered several other potentially serious problems which, at my mother's insistence, they were able to attend to. For once, he was in no position to defy her and she took full advantage of it for his own good.*

*We all breathed a sigh of relief when we knew he was out of danger and back home with mother. The incident, however, had the chilling effect of a rude awakening. Visiting with him as I did each evening, I was shocked to see my "powerhouse" Dad so vulnerable. Though he was hardly a young man at the time, it still cleared the sinuses. For my mother, it was the double shocker of becoming acutely aware of his frailty and dealing with the reality and implications of that frailty on their financial circumstances.*

*The fact was that during his illness, she had been forced to turn down several lucrative jobs that he'd been offered. She'd also blown through much of their savings paying for the medical expenses not covered by insurance. Moreover, it was apparent that he would not be returning to full strength for some indeterminate amount of time. All of this provided a stunning wake-up call and she determined to get matters in hand, beginning immediately.*

*My father made his living as a character actor. He had come to New York City from his family's home in Meriden, Connecticut as a young man to* pursue a career in the theater. If success is measured by following one's heart and always doing for a living what one loves most, then my dad was a great success. He spent pretty much his entire adult life doing just what he set out to do, enjoying a career as an actor. He began by touring the country with a Shakespearean troop, performing different roles each day of the week. When radio was the rage, he would race from studio to studio doing multiple characters on several shows each day. When I was growing up, it was normal to see him on TV in a soap opera or on Phil Silver's "Bilko." There were always various TV commercials running and occasionally he'd land a Broadway or an off-Broadway role.

He loved his work when he was working. Sometimes, however, there were long stretches between jobs and during these times, his job became finding the next job. He called it, "making the rounds." Day after day, he would drive into Queens from our Long Island home and take a subway into the city. He'd spend the day dropping in on agents, producers and casting directors to make sure they knew he was available in case an opportunity came up for a role that he could play. He had tremendous range and could handle many different types of characters. He was a master of make-up and voices. He could speak with many accents, had a decent singing voice and was even known to have a nifty soft-shoe when necessary.

Still, there were many long dry-spells over the years when work seemed extra hard to come by. He remained resolute during these times, however, believing that a great new role was just a call away. Yet the stress could build as the belt would tighten. When he was not working, Dad would collect "unemployment insurance." The regulations were that one had to work at least 26 weeks the prior year in order to be eligible to collect in the current year.

That 26 week hurdle became the bogey that he felt he had to make each year in order to assure that we'd at least have the unemployment insurance the following year if things got rough. This concern led to his accepting jobs in shows that were embarking on tours around the country. They could provide three or four months of work at good pay and cover a big chunk of those 26 weeks. They also, however, took him away from home *for those same long stretches of time. When that occurred, we missed him terribly. We'd anxiously await his lengthy daily letters, which my mother would share with us at dinner each evening.*

*It was a yo-yo existence and caused me, early in life, to seek ways to earn my own money so I would not be a drain on my mother as she tried to juggle family expenses. She'd save up while he was working so it would be available when needed. Somehow, they did it. All three of us survived youth, graduated from college and set about building our lives. However, although there were some serious flirtations, none of us ended up choosing the theater as a career.*

*Now my mother was faced with her greatest fiscal challenge. Her champion, who had managed to churn out a living over the years in a business in which few are able to do so, had suddenly displayed his vulnerability. In addition, pension protection was minimal and his future income producing potential was, more than ever, uncertain. She resolved to take charge.*

*Thankfully, his recovery was remarkably quick. It coincided with a hot streak during which he landed a series of lucrative TV commercials, which I'd swear, she virtually willed him to get. She established a stringent savings and investment program and cut their expenses to the absolute minimum. She proceeded to stash every cent she could get her hands on in "the program."*

*One day when I was visiting, my dad was lamenting the fact that his cronies (note: competition) were starting to die off and that when he now went for an audition, the field had narrowed considerably. I can remember my mother saying, "Yes dear, it must be hard on you to be seeing your pals dropping like flies," while at the same time looking at me out of the corner of her eye with a big sigh of relief. The next five years were actually the most prosperous of their lives. She stuck faithfully with her plan, socking away the bucks.*

*By the time the first bout of cancer struck my dad, she had accumulated enough money to generate income sufficient to cover their expenses. Combined with social security they were okay, and not a moment too soon. Though he recovered for a time and actually had some notable success, within two years he was gone.*

*On his last night, I was alone with him in his least favorite place, a hospital room! Occasionally he'd grip my hand and motion with his eyes for me to put my ear to his mouth, as he could barely muster the strength to speak. His last words to me were that he loved me and I was a great son, but that it was about time that I started behaving more respectfully to him, his usual way of joking with me. When I looked in his eyes and told him that at last I agreed, there was a last discernible sparkle. Then he was gone.*

*My mother was having her own physical challenges at the time and hadn't been able to come to the hospital. When I walked through the door, after I had pulled myself together to tell her the news, she looked at me, smiled sweetly and said, "He's gone, isn't he?" "Yes, Mom," was all I could muster. "I know," she said. "I felt him go about an hour ago. Something inside of me shuddered, and I knew. What will I do now?"*

*"Well," I said. "First you'll get better and then we'll figure it out. We don't need to do anything right now. For the moment, we'll just send lots of love to Dad. What's next will come clear in due time." I told her I was going to call my sisters and started to move toward the phone.*

*"At least, my dear son," she said. "I won't be a burden on you or your sisters. Your wonderful father left me in fine shape. Who would have thought that gypsy would do it, but he did. He was a wonderful guy, your father."*

*"I know, Mom," I said as I dialed.*

# A Thought: *Ride Or Crash*

*A wave breaking on the beach*
*Can lift one in a thrilling rush of power*
*And hurtle them toward the shore*
*Only to deposit them*
*Gently on the sandy beach*

*Or...*

*Slam them to the bottom*
*With a thunderous crash*
*All depending on the degree of harmony*
*Of that one's interaction with it*

*So it is with all aspects of life*
*And each relationship*
*One may experience*

# The Basic Idea

Each and every *action*, whether thought, word or deed that a person may choose to express, has an important input into what quality of *reaction* that individual will attract in return. The predominant nature of those thoughts, words and deeds creates that individuals' own personal and unique mental atmosphere. This atmosphere acts like a magnetic field attracting to that individual its corresponding experience.

Moment to moment, hour by hour, and day by day, each person is continually engaged in the process of making choices. What to do, how to feel or react, what to say and how to say it. Perhaps the most significant characteristic (gift) possessed by all human beings is the ability, in a moment of clarity, to change the quality of those choices, leading to a shift in their mental atmosphere and subsequently, a change in the quality of what is brought into their lives.

*This freedom of choice is what distinguishes humans from all other living creatures.*

At the most fundamental level, each individual selects what they spend their time thinking about, saying, eating, doing, and more. Sometimes the choice is to not choose for themselves at all, but rather, to be led by the opinions and beliefs of others. This is a capitulation of one's basic, most fundamental and most important human quality. Yet the pressure from family and culture can be stifling and repressive.

*Still, all of life operates according to Laws of Nature, which are totally impartial. They merely respond to the input that they are presented with. Actions expressed through an individual's unique freedom of intelligence which are in accordance with the laws of nature, produce harmonious results. Actions expressed with no regard for the law in question may produce chaotic and erratic results, which can be perceived as bad luck, but in actuality, merely represent the law responding to the input it has received.*

Would a chemist try to create carbon dioxide by combining elements other than carbon and oxygen? Perhaps, but if so, it is certain that something other than carbon dioxide would be produced. The chemist, physicist, biologist, carpenter, plumber, lawyer, doctor, chef, mason, painter, musician, and the rest work hard to understand the *principles* of the *laws* that regulate their particular area of interest. The attitudes and actions we then choose to express through the exercise of our *freedom of intelligence* determine the success of our endeavors.

A four year old girl was asked to explain how electricity was able to light up her room. "Easy", she replied. "All you have to do is walk over to the light and flip on the switch. " She was, of course, correct on a rather superficial level. It does indicate, however, that while some laws of life can be quite obvious, others are more subtle.

It is not an easy matter for any individual to discern and acknowledge their own causal role in what happens to them in all areas of their life. Conversely, it is quite easy to place the blame or credit on someone or something outside of one's self, thereby obfuscating an important truth. Namely, the power to bring about change in one's experience through the exercise of one's freedom of choice.

The history books are filled with endless references to each era's attempt to deal with these difficult to discern subtleties. The Greeks and Romans had their gods to explain life's challenges and mysteries. The great religions of the world all have their rituals and interpretations of their particular sacred literature. Yet most are an attempt to place causation outside of the individual for what happens in life, when in fact what really occurs is – *what goes around comes around.*

A loving, yet wizened grandmother I once knew was known to say: "You made your own bed, now you can lie in it."

Another of her favorites was: "Well, dear, now you'll get the chance to stew in your own juice. I wonder how you'll like it?"

The true meaning of these age-old bromides and what she meant to say to her young grandson was that I had created the situation I found myself in and I was going to have to deal with it.

Most people, at one time or another in life, acknowledge to themselves that whatever jam they happen to be in at the moment is of their own doing. Most then pull themselves together and do what is necessary to fix the situation as best they can. Oft-times, however, this realization only arises when dealing with very obvious crisis situations. In truth though, it is applicable to every condition and relationship present in one's life, and is explained by the basic law of life, *The Law of Cause and Effect*. It can be described as follows:

- For every cause there is an equal effect.
- There can be no cause without the attendant effect.
- There can be no effect without the attendant cause.
- In human experience, cause is defined as the *quality of one's thoughts, words and actions.*
- Effect is defined as the *quality of one's life experience, relationships, prosperity, health, etc.*
- In order to improve the *Effect* side of the Law, the *Cause* side must be appropriately altered.
- Human beings are the only living creatures on earth capable of exercising *freely expressed intelligence* to determine for themselves what the quality of their "*Cause*" will be.

The process of grasping this truth and then applying it moment by moment in life is a completely individual matter and can only be accomplished by each person for themselves. In the end, nobody can choose which thoughts another will think, which words they will say, or ultimately, what they will do. Making their own choices is challenge enough. Just ask my Uncle Rabe…

# A Story About Uncle Rabe

*Edwin Rabe was a close family friend who I grew to know and love dearly. He was a man who devoted his life to helping people. Those close to him always referred to him affectionately by his last name (sounds like Robbie). When he was a young man, he taught in a church school for quite a few years. During that time, as was the custom, he lived with a family who were members of the congregation. In his case, that was my dad's family. Over time, Rabe became a devoted member of the family and actually took care of my Grandmother until her death many years later. As for my sisters and myself, he was Uncle Rabe.*

*During WWII, Rabe worked tirelessly to help families new to this country get acclimated to their new homes. He often did without food himself so that some family's children would eat. Everyone in the city knew this man as a kind and gentle person and he was loved by all. He was a very good man. In later years, he began teaching children who had learning disabilities and eventually became the head of the special education program for the entire city where he lived.*

*Then it happened. On his seventy-fifth birthday, he was told he would have to retire from teaching. The law apparently didn't allow anyone to teach in the city school system after reaching 75 years old. He said, "But I'm not too old to teach. I'm still energetic enough and I don't want to retire." Sorry, was the answer.*

*Our gentle friend became very angry and just couldn't accept what had happened. He became embittered toward the very people and school system he'd loved for so long. Soon he became sick and was taken to the hospital. Several months after that, it was discovered that he had cancer. One year later, he died.*

*A few days before his death, I sat at Rabe's bedside and held his hand. He was very weak but had the strength to say a few words to me. "My boy, if you ever get angry, resentful, or jealous, try like heck to stop yourself. I know the reason I'm here today about to die. It's because of all my anger toward the school. I could have found something productive to do, but all I did was sit and think about how much I hated them and how they had done me a dirty deed. Now this is the price I'm paying. Please learn from this and don't ever have to pay this price yourself."*

*He told me he was grateful that he'd realized what he'd done so he could forgive everyone before he died. He'd had a wonderful life he told me, and didn't want it to end in bitterness. Those last few days told the story. Nearly half the city came by the hospital to express their love for him, which gave him great happiness at the end.*

What Uncle Rabe taught me is something that I'll never forget. Thoughts of anger, resentment, envy, and unforgivingness are powerful forces even capable of causing physical disease. Not for the person who caused the anger, but for the one feeling it! Thank you Uncle Rabe, for that powerful lesson.

# The Power of Collective Mind

This brings us to a point that challenges a lot of what's been said before, but requires clarification if one is to really *get it!* Because we must realize that changing one's embedded modes of belief and behavior is far from easy. In fact, it is one of life's toughest tests. It is a process at which even the most successful and enlightened of individuals fail on a regular basis. This is because there is no such thing in this lifetime as finally arriving at perfection. Rather:

*What separates successful people, defined as those who attract prodigious quantities of health, joy, love and prosperity from the rest, is not that they cease to fail, but when they do fail, they put forth the effort and focus to get back on track more quickly.*

They do so because at some point in their lives, they learned that their conscious, on purpose ability to grasp control of their own causative inputs was their greatest gift. They may have never thought about it or articulated it in those terms, but on some level they knew it. Most importantly, it is something that every person can know and get better at applying in their day-to-day life.

The question is, *why is this such a challenge?* A friend who was reviewing an early version of this material said, "Hey, this is all very interesting and the stories are great, but at this point in life, how am I supposed to figure out why I think, feel, believe and do what is either good or not so good for my life? Don't these things become so deeply embedded that usually a person just reacts without thought? How am I supposed to contend with these things?"

It is the $64 billion question. In fact, while my friend was saying a mouthful, he was only scratching the surface of the challenge any individual faces in trying to take charge of life and improve their prospects for greater happiness, health and prosperity. Having said that, it is imperative to try!

*For it is only through that conscious effort that change can occur, making possible a new and better circumstance of life.*

To stay the course, however, it is essential for one to at least understand the forces they are dealing with. While they are formidable, they are by no means beyond the ability of any individual to effectively overcome, given an understanding of their nature and a deep desire to be in the driver's seat of one's own life. They are tricky because they often operate below one's normal level of awareness. They have been referred to as mental influence, race mind, conventional wisdom and other terms. For the purpose of this exercise, they will be referred to as collective mind.

This idea of *Collective Mind* is actually the sum of what can be thought of as distinctly different sources of input including:

- Influences from our tribes, defined as family, friends, peers, teachers, the community, the society.
- Influences from the genes delivered through heredity.

Collective Mind can be found at the heart of every individual and every culture. It explains why equally intelligent people raised in different circumstances emerge into adulthood with ideas, feelings, beliefs and customs which are very different. It describes and explains the predominant ideas of *reality* and a particular culture's ethos or paradigm of life. It is what people know and how they are influenced to behave. It is what is so broadly and individually accepted by a particular society or community that it is often rendered beyond questionability.

Collective Mind is acquired during the period that can be referred to as the pre-critical or prior-to-judgment stage. This is the childlike state in which one assumes and accepts whatever the primary adult authority figures in their world tell them is true. It results in a powerful grip on their belief system for the rest of their life.

Children grow up hearing what their parents, grandparents, teachers, ministers, the media, and all other external influences tell them about themselves, the people around them, the world they live in and how it works.

All of it contributes to one's own belief system which can be defined as, *what one accepts as true about themselves and their life.*

As Voltaire observed, "Every person is a creature of the age in which they live. Very few are able to raise themselves above the ideas of the time."

Likewise, Oliver Wendell Holmes opined, "We are all tattooed in our cradles with the beliefs of our tribe." It is a force whose power is incalculable.

Still, it is only a part of the causation that is referred to here as collective mind.

Another primary source is comprised of *what each individual comes in with.* It does not spring from personal experience or the impress of environment. It consists rather of content which has not been individually accumulated, but that derives from what is passed on genetically from prior generations.

Human behavior and beliefs are driven by the combined action of these two influences. The latter provides a particularly tricky challenge because it is one of those subjects where the veil comes down and nobody can truly explain. Likewise, it is pure conjecture for anyone, including myself, to claim insider information about it.

Yet it also is a subject that we intuitively know is a factor, however shrouded in the fog, in who we are. However, one need not accept this notion to agree that we do have embedded beliefs and reactions that are not easily explainable.

What appears to be an instinctive reaction can often be traced back to *collective mind.* It is what leaves an individual with no explanation for their behavior other than to say, *"That's just the way I am"* or *"That's just how I was raised."* It is a crucial and fundamental element of *self,* that any individual striving for greater freedom must first become aware of, if minimizing its controlling influence is to become an attainable goal.

Lack of such awareness renders one like a prizefighter in the ring, with an opponent they can't see. They have trained hard in preparation, eaten and slept properly, and worked on their jab, hook and upper-cut! Yet now in the ring, it is all rendered ineffectual. They flail around, knowing that somewhere nearby is a force to be reckoned with, but unable to fathom its power or whereabouts!

The fact is, that even when exposed to the light of scrutiny and conscious examination, the grip of *collective mind* is considerable, requiring steadfast determination to break free of *mindless reaction*. Thankfully, there are countless examples of those who have done so and there are myriad prescriptions for achieving that quest. One practical and simple step in that direction is discussed further on. It is important to put into practice, because the fact is:

*Either*
*You Control*
*Your Life*
*Or...*
*The Opinions*
*And Beliefs*
*Of Others*
*Will Gladly Do It*
*For You!*

The following story illustrates just how true this is. It also points out the success that is possible when an individual declares their personal freedom to blaze their own trail out of darkness of mindless manipulation.

# A Story About Miriam

*An article published several years ago in the* New York Times *provides an illustration of both the powerful effect of collective mind and the ability of an individual to emerge from its grip. The story was about a woman named Miriam Wilngal from the mountain village of Minj in Papua New Guinea. It is the only account herein about someone I don't actually know first hand, but it is so inspiring that I feel as if I'd known Miriam for my whole life - or at least wished that was the case.*

*As the story goes, someone in Miriam's clan killed the leader of another clan. This set in motion a demand for compensation that followed a complex tribal calculus. It ended up requiring payment of $15,000, 25 pigs and an 18-year old woman, namely Miriam. Mind you, this is a story that unfolded, not in the 1690's but in the 1990's.*

*It is also important to note that when this story took place, Papua New Guinea had been an independent nation for more than 20 years and had a constitution which recognized the equality of women. Yet it had only been a few decades since the tribes that populate the remote mountains there discovered that they were not the only people on earth, and the customs which allowed Miriam to be thought of as barter to absolve tribal differences were centuries old.*

*Imagine the shock waves that reverberated when Miriam said no, and took off for the capital, Port Moresby, 300 miles to the southeast. There she took refuge from her angry relatives and enlisted the help of a woman Miriam had heard about, who had also broken tradition to become a lawyer. Together they challenged the tribal tradition in court and won a ruling in favor of Miriam, that her rights to personal freedom and equal status had been violated.*

*Paramount are two key ideas. The first is that in this day and age, on this planet, such a mentality could actually not only exist, but be in practice* in the dealings of everyday life. It shows the tremendous power that the collective mind of a particular community exerts on generation after generation, until something or someone revolts from the constraints of it and shocks the system in some way. Secondly, it demonstrates the courage and conviction required to "break out" of those mental bonds. It is nothing short of miraculous that Miriam was able to see beyond the conventional norms of centuries of tradition and actually get herself up and out from under its grip.

Miriam's action becomes even more compelling when one realizes that viewed within the belief system of the country's highland culture, the demand for Miriam as compensation was quite normal. For centuries in Papua New Guinea, women were at the heart of a complex system of relationships based on what was called the "botanical concept of growth."

The mother was known as the "base" of the family tree, her children her "cuttings" or "transplants," her brothers, their uncles called "root people" and the father with no blood tie to the family. When a girl was given in marriage, the family of her husband received the bounty of a "cutting" from the maternal base and acquired an obligation to her brothers which must be repaid. When a generation has passed, according to tribal custom, one or more of her granddaughters were expected to be returned to her family, in a tradition known as "returning the skull in a net bag," or simply "head pay."

The Times article quoted a professor at the University of Papua New Guinea at the time, who held a doctorate from Cambridge University in Britain. He said that regardless of his education, he justifies this practice as a social custom, something referred to by anthropologists as "prescriptive cross-cousin marriage." It is not, he pointed out, much different from the marriage system of European royalty. On the one hand, he viewed Miriam's case with the fascination of a scholar – on the other, he remained a member of the tribe and still lived by its complex code of family traditions.

"I analyze it and I practice it," he said. "I challenge it, but only part of it. There are certain changes we have no choice but to accept, like women's *rights and notions of equality.  But there are certain things that we are compelled to hold onto."*

*Regarding Miriam's situation, he explained, "Yes, a woman is treated as a commodity, but in a spiritual sense it is much more than that.  A woman is an object, but she is a divine object.  I would do the same," he says.  "I have maternal uncles.  I have a daughter.  I must repay the debt of all the work my mother did.  One way is to make the payment in a lump sum and give my daughter back in marriage."  He depicted Miriam's case as, "one which strikes at the root of things, kinship on trial."*

While it may be difficult to understand how a Cambridge-educated Ph.D. could subscribe to such a view, he did so with absolute conviction. In fact, how is the certainty of his belief all that different from the blind acceptance that millions of various religious and cultural adherents have – ideas conceived of and articulated by some individual, possibly centuries ago, often accompanied by claims of divine inspiration, which eventually over time become accepted by their proponents as, "The Gospel!"

Apparently, at some point in time in Papua New Guinea's distant past, someone dreamed up the *botanical concept of growth*, and ever since, democracy or not, constitution or not, people have abided by it faithfully. That is, until Miriam Wilngal unleashed the powerful torrent of individual consciousness rising above the restricting, controlling and conforming power of collective mind.

Lest one catches themselves being amazed by this tale, it is important to point out how easy it is for most people to see the folly of some other person or culture for their seemingly peculiar beliefs, while at the same time clinging to and engaging mindlessly in their own. The key is to examine the source and content of one's own beliefs.

Like Miriam before her awakening, most people think their feelings, ideas, fears, longings, frustrations, etc., are unique to them. What one eventually learns, however, is that not only are they not unique, they are in fact endemic to many in the population – that is, the population of one's particular community, tribe, town, state, religion, nation, et al.

Visit another place on the planet and the set of beliefs, concerns, and customs most prevalent may be quite different.

As individuals, we are subject to the very powerful influence, referred to here as *Collective Mind*. It comprises the backdrop to much of our lives. What are the prevailing religious beliefs? What are the dress codes? What about the norms of cuisine, architecture, sports, literature, music? How many births per family is typical – and deaths by cancer, venereal disease, automobile accidents, drownings, crib deaths, plane crashes? What sort of education or economic opportunities are available? What is read in the newspaper or seen on TV news reports? Add to these the binding imprint of inherited influences we cannot even fathom.

All of these factors contribute to a virtual barrage on your belief systems about your place in the world – what you are supposed to do and believe – how you're expected to behave and perform – what sort of freedom or lack thereof you can expect – what the future may hold.

As such, much of what you think, say, and do is driven by factors and influences that you may not be conscious and aware of. It could in fact be said that:

*You are truly your own person only to the degree that you are able to consciously pick and choose which elements of the collective mind that have shaped you, that you wish to retain and which you would prefer to replace – and do replace.*

This is no small feat, particularly in an environment that applies pressure to adhere to cultural norms and not rock the boat! It also presupposes that you even understand and agree with this assessment – and have the desire to create your own standards and reality.

However that shakes out, to the degree that you do not exercise your freedom to choose, through either acquiescence or simple lack of awareness, you do become subject to what may be termed *The Law of Averages*. What you accept as being just a part of life will become embedded as part of life. The one who accepts themselves as a statistic, most likely ends up a statistic, surely the case for most of us.

# A Thought: *The Boiling Pot*

*Since time began*
*words to live by*
*have been suggested*
*by thoughtful people*

*courage, responsibility, faith, kindness*
*honesty, caring, goodness*

*Regardless of such high ideals*
*the world is always in turmoil*

*There may never have been a time*
*when all the people of the earth*
*agreed at the same time*
*to live by words like these*

*Yet how wonderful*
*my world would be*
*if only I could stick to them*
*all the time*

# The Electrician and the Law

We live in a very interesting world. It is one that combines *freely expressed intelligence* with *very specific law*. Each individual has the freedom to use their intelligence to select the course they follow, but each is also subject to the laws of nature.

*Because these laws are absolutely specific, they can always be counted on.*

An apprentice electrician is someone in the process of uncovering and understanding the various principles of the law of electricity. He is not trying to invent the law. It is impossible to invent something which has always existed. It was already there long before it was recognized as such by the human race. He is, rather, trying to comprehend what already is, so that he may better use its power successfully.

*It is exactly what you are trying to do by reading this.*

When the apprentice considers which actions to take in order to achieve a particular goal, he uses his intelligence freely. As his understanding grows and he discovers how the *law of electricity* works, he confirms what already exists. To become a successful master electrician, he must ultimately learn how to harmonize his freely expressed intelligence and actions with *the law* he is putting to use.

The master electrician knows the foolishness of trying to get around the law. He would no more consider short cuts than sticking his finger in an electrical socket. He very clearly knows the price. His healthy and unquestioning respect for the principles of the law of electricity, combined with his freely expressed intelligence, result in a harmonious combination of humanity with an important law of nature.

Consider the foolish apprentice who does try to circumvent principles of electricity, in order to cut corners. Obviously, a price will be paid for that action. The apprentice will either learn from the experience or find some other line of work. He has the freedom to intelligently choose his course of action, but if he insists on choosing a way that conflicts with the principles of the law, then he will clearly not be very successful as an electrician.

The master works hard to understand the law, and then to intelligently choose courses of action which capture the law's power, making it work for them rather than against them. Only fools continue to use their freedom to make choices which conflict with the principles they have learned.

There is not a person who ever lived who wouldn't be able to think of many examples of their own foolishness. It is part of the human condition and recognizing that is an essential ingredient in personal growth. It is from these experiences that each individual is able to realize the impact they have on their own lives and learn to make more intelligent choices. More important than the errors of judgment are the ensuing changes that hopefully occur as understanding grows.

The real issue is whether an individual is able to grasp the *principles* of the *laws of life* and then, like the master electrician, use their *freedom of intelligence* to make choices that are in harmony with those principles. To the extent that past errors help move one along in that process, they are valued experiences.

It's actually not a personal matter. The *laws of life* have no bias whatsoever against any particular race, religion, culture, nation, community or individual. They merely exist. They don't treat the rich any better than anyone else. They don't make special provisions for those with PhD's, MBA's or the like. They allow no special exceptions for those born of higher rank and privilege, or the opposite.

Stand by the edge of the harbor in a seaside town and observe the way the water treats the many varieties of boats it supports. What distinction does the water make between the very grand vessels and the smaller, less impressive ones? The answer is none. It floats them all. Survey the scene again following the fury of a hurricane. Which boats did the storm designate to be spared from the devastation?  Again the answer is none.

Similarly, the law of gravity does not employ selectivity when determining who to subject to its force.  We all are.  Nor does the rain select one farm to nourish and another to deny.  In fact, a garden will respond as readily to a peasant as to the richest of persons depending on the quality of cultivation they employ.

If these laws were variable and changeable depending on circumstances, personality, charm, and the like, the world would collapse into utter chaos.  To the contrary, life operates in perfect order precisely because of the unwavering foundation provided by the Laws that shape it.

We succeed in our lives to the extent that we understand the Laws of Life and adjust our thoughts, words and actions accordingly.

The *Law of Cause and Effect* operates on the same impersonal basis as all other laws. Cause is translated into effect in exact measure.  There is no judgment or discrimination involved.  The Law simply takes the input or cause and produces an effect of the same exact quality. I consider both Vinnie and Melinda to be great examples.

# A Story About Vinny

*In the days before the likes of Uber, Vinny was the guy who picked me up to drive me to or from the airport when I needed a car service. But in a larger sense, Vinny was much more than that as well as an inspirational example of how the world works. I first met Vinny when I was going on a business trip. As was customary, I called the local cab company and requested a car to pick me up at a certain time so I could make an early flight. Waiting for me the next morning was Vinny.*

*He was an engaging fellow with a pleasant manner. He had emigrated from South America and had found his way to the community where I lived. He told me he was working very long hours in order to save money for the time when he'd be ready to strike out on his own. He wasn't sure at the time what it was he'd do, but he knew he wanted to work for himself. After all, he told me, he was getting up there. He'd just turned twenty-six and didn't want to be one of those thirties and forties types he saw all around him who still had nothing to show for their lives.*

*It was not my practice to ask for a particular driver when I called for a car, but after having reliability problems on several occasions, I began requesting Vinny more and more. He told me that the real problem was not always the driver. It was not unusual for the dispatcher to botch the information due to being too busy or in a snit. The real issue, Vinny said, was that the cab company really had the town locked up. They were the only ones allowed to have a facility at the train station and therefore dominated the action. They were literally the only game in town, a virtual monopoly with high rates that nobody could contest, and little incentive to provide top quality service.*

*Most of his business, Vinny told me, was booked directly with his customers. They would call him and leave a message. He would confirm it back to them, arrange his schedule and then inform the cab company about where he'd be and when he'd be available to take calls from them. He offered me his card with his direct phone number, which I gladly accepted.*

*No longer did I have to worry about whether someone would show up to take me to my early flights. If Vinny couldn't make it himself, he'd arrange for another driver to pick me up and make sure he was there on time. It was great. Until the day of the incident. While it was not really that big a deal to me, call it a minor aggravation in the scheme of life, to Vinny it was "the straw".*

*I was returning that day from a trip and had to be picked up at the airport. Due to the weather, it wasn't clear which flight I'd be on, so I left word for Vinny that I'd leave pick-up details for him with the dispatcher once I knew more. There were both upper and lower exits, and which one I chose would depend on whether I checked my bags or carried them on the plane. You know the rigamarole.*

*When things came into focus, I called and asked the dispatcher to tell Vinny to pick me up downstairs by the baggage area.*

*Usually Vinny would have been there, ready to give me a hand with the bags, but this time, no Vinny. Not a problem, I figured. Just gather the bags. He'll be along. I waited, looked around, walked outside to see if he was parked and waiting out there, but he was nowhere in sight. So I called the cab company again. "Where's Vinny?" I asked. "Oh, he's there," the dispatcher replied. "He just called to see if we'd heard from you. He's waiting by the upper exit."*

*There was basically no explanation for why Vinny was not where I had requested him to be. The specific instructions had evidently been omitted from my request form. All I wanted to do was get out of there. I gathered my things and trudged to the escalator. Adding insult to injury, it was out of order, so I lugged everything up the stairs and out the doors. There, waiting for me, was Vinny.*

*In truth, he was more upset than I was and on the ride home I learned a few expletives in Spanish and Portuguese, as Vinny expressed his feelings about his colleagues. When he dropped me off, he told me that he had some ideas and that I'd be hearing from him.*

*It took about three months for me to learn what he meant. When I opened the envelope, I smiled. It contained notice of the formation of a new car service established to provide superior service at a reasonable price. Apparently, there were several drivers who shared Vinny's views and had agreed to join him in his quest for excellence. Like many of his regular customers, I was only too willing to give my business to this new effort. I also enthusiastically recommended Vinny's new enterprise to others. Why not? I was receiving great service at a fair price and helping someone to realize their dream at the same time.*

*I suspect that Vinny will end up with a very successful enterprise.*

*"You know," he told me, "I can't let any more grass grow under my feet. I've wasted enough time. I am almost thirty, you know!"*

# A Story About Melinda

*Melinda was my sales assistant at one point early in my stock brokerage career. A sales assistant is the chief cook and bottle washer – they keep them organized to enable them to concentrate on generating business. Stock brokers are usually compensated by commission. It is a highly competitive business where every commission dollar is hotly contested. As such, the role of the sales assistant is integral to the broker's success.*

*It is a job that in those days, attracted young women with varying degrees of ambition. Then as now, some were content with their role as helper, nursemaid, psychiatrist, organizer, all-purpose supporter. Others see it as a "foot in the door" opportunity, a stepping stone into a business where "producers" can earn substantial incomes. They are willing to put up with their duties in order to get a shot at bigger and better things.*

*Brokers desperately search for the former type and for good reason. It is not easy to find and cultivate a superior sales assistant. It takes time to get comfortable with each other, gain confidence in their abilities, get one's clients used to them, teach them the basics, develop a routine and gain confidence in their abilities. The last thing the broker wants is to go through that process only to have their assistant walk and have to go through it again. Pure nightmare.*

*Working for me may have been Melinda's first job. It was certainly early in her career. She was very bright and eager to learn, but what stood out was her terrific personality. She was quite funny and would frequently dispense amusing off-hand comments. It did not take long, however, to realize that as a sales assistant, Melinda was squarely in the nightmare category which I mean as a well-deserved compliment. At the time, however, I didn't exactly see it that way. I was struggling to establish myself and needed all the help I could get. Playing the role of career counselor* to Melinda was not high on my priority list. But, she was such a great gal and such an obvious misfit.

There is one particular incident which I will never forget. I had made it to the office just in time for the daily 8:00 a.m. morning meeting. Usually I arrived in time to pick up a cup of tea at the in-house snack bar, but a late train had conspired to interfere with the program on this particular day. So, as I settled into my seat, I turned to Melinda and asked her to please run down and pick me up a cup. This was, by the way, a common practice at the time and considered part of the job description.

"Well," she said, "fine, I will. And why don't I wash your socks for you when I return?"

Off she went in a huff. When she did return and found my socks in a ball on her desk, we got a good laugh out of it. It was clear, however and rightfully so, that she had an extreme distaste for any activity that smacked of subservience.

Shortly after that incident, I took Melinda aside and encouraged her to begin studying for the Series 7 examination, the test required to become licensed as a broker. I reasoned that if she weren't working for me, that she would have been long since replaced and that she'd better start preparing to be a broker herself. Also, the company we worked for was supportive of assistants pursuing their Series 7 designation. A few months later, when I left that firm for another opportunity, it was not long before Melinda moved on as well. When she did, however, it was as an official, fully-qualified broker.

Over the years, I had occasion to see or speak with Melinda every now and then. She even handled some business for my mother before she passed away. Her hard work, pleasant manner and ever-present wry sense of humor served her well and she built a terrific business. She served many people who benefitted enormously from her dedicated, straightforward and caring approach to their financial needs.

I recently had occasion, purely coincidentally, to bump into Melinda in the elevator of my office building. She was bubbling over with enthusiasm, as she told me about the new private office her firm had just given her, the kind reserved for the most highly regarded and biggest producers of the firm. She told me with relish about the young man she had just hired to be her new sales assistant.

"So Melinda," I asked her. "Do you ask him to get you your tea?"

"Only drink coffee from Starbucks," she said with a smile.

# A Thought: *Express What You Value*

*Every person appreciates*
*Observing or experiencing*

*Someone who takes pride*
*In what they do*

*And tries their hardest*
*To do their best*
*At whatever*
*Their job may be*

*Everyone also*
*Has their own opportunity*
*Each and every day*

*To give someone else the pleasure*
*Of observing that same*

*Passion and dedication*
*In them*

# The Sole Responsibility Factor

- Whatever a person may achieve in life, whether positive or negative, is the result of that person's thoughts, words, and actions.

- Any individual's points of strength or weakness belong solely to them.

- A person's future circumstances belong to them as well, and emanate from their choices and beliefs.

- As they think, speak, and act, so life presents the matching experiences that will greet them.

- A shift in the quality of those choices will show up in a corresponding shift in the quality of life they experience.

- It all comes down to the choices one makes, from the most fleeting thought to the boldest action.

The significance is that:

- These choices are the major input that determine the quality of our own life.

- By changing the quality of one's choices, one can change the quality of their life.

- In spite of the powerful influence of collective mind, making these changes is within every person's capability.

- It is not possible to do this for anyone else, and each must do it for themselves.

There are many people who expend great quantities of time, energy, and money attending lectures and seminars, reading books, listening to tapes, the whole gamut of self-development activities. They do so in the hope that this participation will improve their lives, and it certainly is a better way to spend their time and money than many alternatives.

But check the results. Does the individual then go back into life and respond in the same old way to situations that confront them, or do they make the effort to change? The truth is that many teachings have good to offer, but it is always up to the individual to put into practice what they've learned.

In the final analysis, one must pro-actively change their own behavior in order to break the grip of the collective mind and begin a new dynamic. Remember, there is nobody on earth who can do that for you, but you. If someone else offers, head for the mirror fast!

The real challenge is changing, in the moment, under the pressure of whatever is happening, the quality of the response (thought, word, or action) that has become *built in*, the default, the automatic pilot. One knows they're on the track when they find themselves saying,

*"I can do better."*

An illustration of this is a man I know who looked in the mirror one day, saw an unpleasantly oversized waistline, and decided to do something about it. Determined, he signed up to attend a lecture-series on weight loss and purchased a stationary bicycle. Then he also purchased a log to record daily caloric intake.

Over the ensuing months, he gained knowledge from the lecture series, the avid consumption of several fascinating books on the subject, and numerous stimulating discussions with others of similar interests, all in preparation for the day he would actually start using the log and the exercise bike. During that period, much to his dismay, his waistline continued to expand.

What finally became crystal clear was that no amount of cycling by the instructor or other participants of the lecture series, or the authors of the books he read, was going to reduce his waistline. Only his energy and discipline, and his alone, finally got the job done.

"You know," he told me one day after he had achieved his goal, "It was really pretty obvious what I had to do, and I really wanted to do it, but oh, it was so hard to actually change my habits. Some days, I felt as though my feet were stuck in tar, and I just wasn't moving."

As of this moment, well over several years later and counting, he' looking good!

The looking good for him, by the way, is not because I or anyone else thought his waistline was too large. It is because he thought so. He wanted to make a change in the *effect* side of the equation. To do so, he first had to make a change in the *cause* side. He had to disrupt his old patterns and install new ones. Until he did, nothing happened. Once he did, the effect was set in motion. Little by little, in increments, positive results followed positive change.

My friend John is a great case study in how this dynamic unfolds in real life.

# A Story About John

*John was always outstanding at whatever activity he pursued. We met in college where, after a shaky start, we became fast friends, a condition still in effect.*

*It was clear at once that John was different. He was very sharp in his appearance and seemed very purposeful in how he went about doing things. The college we attended was part of the New York State University system which was more affordable for kids like us. At the time, attendance meant an automatic major in education. Like me, John started life as an elementary school teacher.*

*Through focus, hard work and dedication, John became an outstanding educator, winning praise and appreciation from his students and their parents as well as several awards for the excellent results his students achieved. If he had stayed in education, he no doubt would be the head of some school district or the president of a university.*

*Due to a particular confluence of events, however, John developed a keen interest in law enforcement. Over a period of time, he became a full-fledged police officer of the town in which he and his family lived. He threw himself into his training and work with great energy and focus and was soon considered the best on the force, often chosen to handle the most challenging situations. Then a new idea emerged.*

*One day a co-worker of John's, who was a recreational pilot, invited John to go for a ride in his single-engine aircraft. In recalling the experience to me at a later time, he described it as awe-inspiring. He set about at once to become a pilot himself. With his usual single-mindedness of purpose, he achieved one rating after another in record time. Before long, he took a second job as a flight instructor so he could build up his flight hours while getting paid. Once he started applying his teaching skills, he became so busy as a flight instructor that he decided to give up his law enforcement career. His love of flying, combined with his commitment and purposeful direction of energy, had him started on the road to finding his true purpose.*

*To augment his flight instruction work, John began accepting assignments to fly corporate clients and eventually went to work for several companies which offered that service. While engaged in this activity, he observed various regulatory abuses that he thought were potentially dangerous and therefore intolerable. His law enforcement background compelled him to report these abuses to the authorities. The fuss he made got him fired from his job, but resulted in severe penalties and corrective action to the company in question. Most importantly, it brought John to the attention of the Federal Aviation Authority, which hired him as an inspector.*

*Today, John is a senior inspector for the F.A.A. His job is to be a watch-dog for potentially dangerous violations of Federal regulations. In this capacity, John has been trained on many types of aircraft, being "forced" to spend many hours flying the equipment. "Hardship duty", he joyfully calls it with a smile. He frequently has to teach mechanics and pilots some of the finer points he has learned and often receives comments about how he would have made a great teacher if he had considered education as a career.*

*Through his diligence, uncompromising demand for safety and strict adherence to regulations, John has also spotted and corrected many situations that could have resulted in disastrous consequences. Many who come in contact with him say he would have made one heck of a cop. He smiles.*

# A Thought: *Chances Keep Coming*

*One of the great mysteries about this life*
*is how many opportunities it presents*
*to lift one's self*
*to a higher level of being*

*Over and over they come*
*regardless of how bad we behave*
*or how tough the circumstances*
*we may find ourselves in*

*The chances relentlessly keep pouring in*
*to turn it around and do the right thing*
*and they won't stop coming*
*right up to the end*

*The question is when does one see*
*what's there for the taking*
*when does one open their eyes*
*and make the decision*
*to follow through*
*and try a better way*

# THE SUBTLE GRADATIONS OF THOUGHTS, WORDS AND ACTIONS

*Cause* has been described as *the quality of one's thoughts, words and actions,* and it has been stated that for each *cause/input,* there is an equal *effect/output* in one's life experience.

Other ways to say it are:

- Every condition or circumstance of one's life is the direct product or result of that individual's cause/input, comprised of their thoughts, words, and actions, combined with the influence of collective mind.

- There is no such thing as good or bad luck. What is seen as luck is actually either the influence on the individual of collective mind or the direct reflection of their cause/input.

- Life can be viewed as a garden. It operates in a manner which is every bit as exact as horticulture but nowhere near as obvious. In a garden, if one plants a rose, one doesn't get a tulip, one gets a rose. If one plants a weed, one also won't get a lovely bloom but rather an undesirable interloper.

- In the human experience, the seeds are thoughts, words and actions. The relevant question then becomes, exactly what kind of garden of life is one planting?

- The fact is that this garden of life will harvest exactly what has been planted, nothing else. It is much easier to recognize the results in one's garden of plants than in one's garden of life, but it works the same way in both.

So far, the discussion of *cause* has dealt mainly with actions. No less important, though more demanding on the comprehension, is the causal power of thoughts and words. It is not true that the act alone has power. Thoughts and words are more subtle forms of the same powerful cause, and they produce the correspondingly more subtle, less obvious response in one's outer world.

This notion causes a great deal of consternation and debate. Nobody wants to think that a word or a thought passing through their mind really has any power. It is almost impossible to deal with because it means that feelings of anger, envy, resentment, and the like, as well as the words that express those feelings, are definite inputs of a negative variety that will show up in some unpleasant way in one's own life.

"Okay, the action is understandable," one might say. "I can see that if I murder someone, I've set myself up to either be killed or spend a long, miserable time in prison. Or, I can see how cheating on an exam, not doing my homework, or beating my children are all actions that set up fittingly unpleasant results. But how can talking about or thinking about those things hurt me?"

Efforts to answer this question have filled many books. It is most clearly embodied, however, by people you have probably known who spend a lot of time and energy in a state of constantly expressing their misery. It may take the form of complaining about some injustice they've suffered, or running critical commentary about the people in their life. Perhaps they overly dwell on hurts and resentments.

Recall the results you observed in those folk's lives. What good came from those activities? It is most likely the answer would be *none!* Who wants to be around someone like that? If one views their own experience with negativity, the same conclusion is likely.

The fact is that while negative words or thoughts may or may not impact the object of their intent, they definitely impact the life of the speaker or thinker. The insidious aspect of words and thoughts is that people, for the most part, are not aware that there are specific consequences to them, determined in exact measure by their quality.

This is not a new idea. Consider the thoughts of several of the great minds of the ages;

*Rule your mind or it will rule you.*
*Horace (65-8 B.C.)*

*The soul becomes dyed with the color of its thoughts.*
*Marcus Aurelius (121-180 A.D.)*

*If you don't have something nice to say, don't say anything at all.*
*My Nana (1875-1952 A.D.)*

And finally, a frightening notion:

*Remember, happiness doesn't depend upon who you are or*
*what you have. It depends solely upon what you think.*
*Dale Carnegie (1888-1955)*

Thoughts are powerful, though subtle, forces. They are powerful enough to remove one's attention, even from a subject that one had chosen to focus on, like a conversation, a lecture, or a play. The mind goes off on a tangent, captured by a thought, and precious moments are lost. Happens to us all. The question is, how much?

| Cause | = | Effect |
|---|---|---|
| Distracting Thoughts | = | Missed Opportunity |

Medical science abounds with examples of the effect of thought on the physical body. Many of the more progressive doctors of our day acknowledge the disease-inducing power of thoughts laced with envy, anger, hatred and bitterness. Conversely, laughter, joy and well-being are now actively pursued as tools for healing all sorts of ills. Thoughtful people are realizing that a person's character is defined by their deep belief system, which in turn is defined by the sum total of their thoughts.

*The mental atmosphere of an individual created by their belief system acts as a magnet, drawing to them experiences affecting in kind their health, happiness and prosperity.*

It is broadly recognized that a good character results from the ongoing generation of good thoughts, words, and actions, just as a lowly character results from the continued dwelling on corrupt thoughts and feelings and subsequent actions. People clearly define their own nature and ensuing life's experience. In the factory of their mind, they create the tools to either build themselves up or tear themselves down.

So the question for us all is – when you consider the predominant patterns of thoughts, words and actions that you choose or allow yourself to engage in, what sort of tools are you creating? What's the answer? It is important to take seriously, and has been alluded to many times, but most famously by the poet William Ernest Henley, in the last two lines of his brilliant "Invictus," when he wrote:

> *"I am the master of my fate:*
> *I am the captain of my soul."*

Each of us is the master and shaper of our own life experience through either exercising our freedom to chose our thoughts, words and actions, or failing to do so. Either way, it is the individual's choice, not that of some far off deity, or parent, or spouse, or sibling. You take control when you accept your own causal responsibility and adjust your thoughts, words and actions accordingly.

Consider the following:

- An individual doesn't suddenly commit some terrible action after living a wonderful life. Such action was most likely preceded by a long series of dishonorable or immoral thoughts that gathered energy until the right moment presented itself. The action was not in isolation. Had the thought pattern been changed, the action would never have occurred.

- An individual's outer world of appearance, conditions and circumstance is shaped by the influence of the collective mind on their thoughts, words and actions.

- The individual who is master to their thoughts, words, and actions is truly master of their life, as one attracts the equivalence of what one expresses through those thoughts, words and actions.

- Some people choose goals that are good but continuously torpedo those aims by allowing themselves to indulge in thoughts, words, and actions that are not supportive of them.

- People may be anxious to improve the effect (circumstances and conditions of their life), but may be unwilling to change the cause (thoughts, words, and actions) accordingly. Ultimately, each individual achieves their objectives when they are in sync with the *causal* action they project.

- Just as negative causes produce the same effects, so do positive inputs, or causes, produce equally positive effects. As the saying goes, *like attracts like*. This is clearly understood in the physical world of nature. It is less understood in the world of human experience, but is just as simple and exact in the mechanics of how it works.

- The individual who grasps the concept of *The Law of Cause and Effect* and takes control of their causal input will be shocked at how quickly important, positive changes will appear in their life.

- People usually think that their thoughts are their exclusive and private domain. This is not the case.

*Negative thoughts breed equally base words and actions which produce a corresponding condition of misery. Likewise, thoughts, words and actions of a high quality produce conditions of peace, health, success and prosperity.*

Consider my friend, Spencer.

# A Story About Spencer

*Of all the guys I have known and been close to, Spencer is one of those I have really looked up to – sort of like the big brother I never had. At first I was simply awestruck by his athletic ability. In fact, I still am. Our first athletic competition was on a tennis court. I was thirty or so and he was a few years older. Tennis was my game. I played several times a week, and kept my racquet and tennis clothes in my car at all times, so I'd always be ready on the spur of the moment, just in case a game appeared. I'd started playing in college, too late for a serious game, but amongst weekend players, I was dangerous.*

*Spencer and I had met earlier that day. We were on vacation – he with his wife, Laurie, and me with my girlfriend – at a resort in the Dominican Republic. Bonnie and I had finished breakfast and were playing a game of backgammon when Spencer ambled over to watch. We all introduced ourselves and he began to kibitz about our game, taking special umbrage at the strategy suggested by some of my moves.*

*Sensing the rising heat, Bonnie said, "Spencer, why don't you and Rob play a game? I want to do some reading."*

*"Great. I mean, if that's okay with you Rob."*

*"Let's do it." I answered.*

*Remarkably, Spencer's comments about my backgammon prowess continued throughout our game. After each of my moves, he would intone his view of its obvious inadequacy and embellish on what could have been achieved otherwise. Nor did my victory in that and each subsequent game we played dim his ardor for critical analysis. On the contrary, when we concluded, he opined that there were just times when pure luck could overcome even the most obvious lack of skills.*

On face value, one might ask why anyone would ever speak with such an obnoxious individual again, much the less become lifelong friends. The fact is, though, that I had so much fun winning those games, and Spencer's commentary was laced with such a smirky and amusing locker room type of humor that the question never occurred to me, and best friends it has been ever since.

When the backgammon ended we sat around chatting for a while. Laurie joined us and the conversation turned to the upcoming U.S. Open and who had the best chance. Would Connors prevail? How about Borg or Vilas, McEnroe or Lendl? Eventually the question was asked.

"Do you play, Rob?"

"Oh, a bit. How about you?"

"Spencer is a pretty good player, Rob," Laurie added, as if sensing what was happening.

"Oh, how long have you been playing, Spencer?" I asked.

"Started when I got back from Vietnam. Laurie worked at Columbia so I got to play at their tennis facility. I've cut back quite a lot, but maybe we can hit some later."

Well, how bad could it be, I thought? He started playing about the same time in life that I did. Nothing to be concerned about.

"How about four this afternoon?" I suggested.

"Great!"

Turns out that Spencer was a different caliber athlete than I was used to encountering. In high school, he was one of the starting pitchers in the New York City all-star game at Yankee Stadium and was considered a top school-boy "prospect" by major league scouts. He'd received a full athletic scholarship to St. John's University for baseball and basketball. He was the starting guard on the great teams of the Connie Hawkins era. In fact, even today in his late 60's, Spencer can hit 85 to 90 out of 100 foul shots and swish jumpers from beyond the arc at will.

*A devastating shoulder injury had put a premature end to college and dreams of a professional athletic career. Moreover, war was going full blast, and off to Vietnam he went. Luckily he returned, began his career and most importantly, met his future wife.*

*Laurie had grown up in a tennis playing family. In fact, her brother was a teaching pro. Spencer had taken to the game and thrown himself into it. He played every possible day he could, and soon began entering amateur tournaments. Laurie's Columbia connection played an important role as Spencer became friendly with the coach, who was an ex-player on the professional tour. He encouraged Spencer to work out with the team in order to provide his players with competition. Spencer was soon providing more than most of them could handle. His amateur ranking climbed rapidly as Spencer's tournament results surged. He became regarded as one of the top players in his age group.*

*I arrived at the tennis court at a little before 4:00 P.M. that afternoon. Spencer was already there practicing serves. We greeted each other and began to rally. I noticed, somewhat alarmingly, that the harder I would hit the ball to Spencer, the harder it would come back. What's more, it didn't seem to matter whether I was hitting to his forehand or his backhand. That was a bit disconcerting since most of the people I played with including myself, had much weaker backhands. Still, I soon got into a groove and was hanging in there. It was probably the best practice session of its kind that I'd ever experienced. Then it ended.*

*"So Rob. Would you like to play a few games?"*

*"Um... ah... sure," I responded.*

*"Great. Why don't you serve first?"*

*"Whew!" I thought. "What a break."*

*Spencer obviously didn't know that my serve was the strongest part of my game. We'd been practicing ground strokes, so he hadn't seen any. I was pretty proud of my serve. It had won a lot of matches for me and I had more confidence in it than any other stroke. It was in fact, my most commonly recurring tennis fantasy that if my first serve was on, even Jimmy*

*Connors would have trouble returning it. So for sure, I'd take Spencer by surprise in the first game at least, and put the pressure on him when he had to serve to me.*

*I stepped up to the line to serve.*

*"Here goes," I yelled.*

*"Good game," he called back.*

*I was elated when I connected solidly with that first shot. The ball screamed over the net, landing in the far corner of the server's box.*

*"Ace," I thought ...then... "What? Hey!!" as his cross-court return flew by my lunging racquet.*

*"Great serve, Rob. I just got lucky on that one," Spencer offered.*

*"Wow, great return," I lamely replied.*

*Oh my word, what a thrashing. Somehow I managed to get a game out of each of the three sets we played that day, due primarily, I suspect, to Spencer's good sportsmanship. In our dinner conversation that evening, he referred to our match in terms of, "all the great points" we'd played.*

*Laurie smiled. "Don't worry, Rob. You actually did really well. You stuck it out for three sets. Spencer rarely finds someone at a place like this who lasts more than one, unless it's the pro. Even then, they usually don't last more than two. But Rob, just a hint. The next time you plan a game of tennis with Spencer, try to remember not to bring out the backgammon game first."*

*"Now ya tell me," I frowned, as we all had a good laugh.*

*When we returned from that vacation, Spencer and I stayed in touch, in time becoming good friends. Slowly, I learned about why sports had played such a prominent role in his life. Spencer and his brother Jerry had grown up in Brooklyn, New York, the sons of troubled parents. Their mother had severe mental and emotional problems and she spent much of their early years in various city institutions. Their father was unable to cope and the boys spent a big chunk of their formulative years in a "Boy's Home" with little parental guidance or influence. Sports were Spencer's refuge.*

When he returned home from Vietnam, he had begun his career, married Laurie and started playing tennis. Success had followed in all areas, but dark clouds were brewing. Perhaps it was the birth of his daughter, Victoria and the need to confront his own personal experience with parenthood that kicked it off, but for whatever reason, things started to shift. The euphoria of Victoria's birth gave way to the realities and restrictions of a new baby. Spencer and Laurie began experiencing tremendous stress in their marriage. Business for the first time in all his working years seemed to be undergoing a downturn. All of a sudden he started getting hit with stomach problems.

Over the next couple of years Spencer's decline accelerated. Health problems plagued him, making any athletic activity extremely difficult. The business he had built so successfully declined to the point where he was forced to shut it down and look for a job. His income plummeted. He was compelled to liquidate assets he had acquired and cut way back on expenditures. Somehow, he and Laurie clung together. All I could do was observe what was happening and be there as a friend, but it was during this time that I found out what Spencer was really made of.

What most impressed me about Spencer was his approach to overcoming his woes. He studied. He became a voracious consumer of philosophical examinations of life. He took classes about how to live effectively, about parenting and marriage. He learned how to moderate his emotional swings and frustrations through the practice of meditation. Not to say that things improved all that quickly. Even Andrew's birth was a two-edged sword. On one hand, a cause for great joy. On the other, more concern for how he could handle the responsibility for yet another, when he still had so much to overcome himself. Yet on he struggled.

There is no particular moment when a clear shifting of fortune was apparent, no clear line of delineation when things turned upwards. But like a giant ship turning in the ocean, a sea change took place in Spencer's life and the results today are stunning. His marriage to Laurie and his love and appreciation of her are stronger than ever. Victoria is a lovely young lady, an accomplished musician and now a mother herself. Andrew is a terrific *young man and surprise, surprise, an outstanding athlete. Business-wise, Spencer is on the way to another record year. He still has health issues, but he keeps them under control. What a turnabout.*

*I find it interesting that while there is this competitive element to our friendship, there is definitely a deep and brotherly aspect as well. In fact most of our time together is spent discussing our lives, challenges, defeats, triumphs, etc. While I have other friends with whom I also discuss life's issues, the intellectual depth of my interactions with Spencer transcend them all. He is clearly the most open, the most thoughtful, and the most knowledgeable person I know. The fact that he has experienced trauma, had his life shaken to the core and worked long and hard to "right his ship," goes a long way toward explaining why!*

There are people who go through a lot less than Spencer did, and end up losing their families, job, home and more. To his credit, Spencer hung in, adjusted his automatic reactions to challenges, set a new course, and changed the trajectory of his life. I attribute that to the high quality of his response to his challenges, which is not to suggest that he's home free. He certainly can't afford to rest on his laurels now that circumstances have improved. On the contrary, his very life story is a testament to his need to keep at it. Well-equipped from his years of study and bolstered by his front row view of the results, however, it is my opinion that he will stay on course. Of course, as with us all, it is now and will always be a work in progress!

# A Thought: *Thoughts Lead the Way*

*Watch your thoughts;*
*they become words.*
*Watch your words;*
*they become actions.*
*Watch your actions;*
*they become habits.*
*Watch your habits;*
*they become character.*
*Watch your character;*
*it becomes your destiny.*

*Frank Outlaw*

# A Story About Jerry

*My first real business job was with the advertising agency, Benton & Bowles. I had decided that teaching public school was just too limiting. I yearned to find out what life was like for the people in suits I'd see leaving and returning from New York City on the train each day. I longed to be compensated for my individual ability, drive and achievement, something unavailable in public education.*

*One summer day, I picked up the classified section of the New York Times and circled ads. My very first appointment was with an employment agency looking to fill a public relations job. When I met the counselor, however, he said he'd just received a call on another job which might be perfect for me. That afternoon, I met with Howard at Benton & Bowles, and the next day I had the job. Just like that! And at a healthy increase from what I was earning as a teacher. The principal I worked for expressed regret about losing me, but I was psyched to move on.*

*The next year was exciting and fast paced. I worked on products from General Foods, Procter & Gamble, Vick Chemical and others. The job entailed meeting with clients, determining their objectives and needs, then coming up with a strategy to help achieve them. At first, I tagged along with Howard and other more senior members of the group. Before long, I caught on with some of the clients and started carrying the ball on my own.*

*Then one day, out of the blue, Howard walked in and said he was resigning to pursue an opportunity at Lever Brothers. I was in shock. I liked Howard very much. He was a nice guy and he had endeavored sincerely to teach me the business. He was my first official business mentor and he was leaving. My concerns were allayed somewhat when Howard's boss, Bill, assured me that my work and progress were recognized and appreciated. He told me that I should not be concerned about my future at Benton & Bowles. Relieved, I eagerly helped in the organization of a good-bye party for Howard.*

*All during the time I'd been at B&B, I had heard stories about a guy who had worked for the department before I had arrived on the scene. In fact, his leaving to join another agency had created the opening which I had filled. His name was Jerry and he had created quite a legend in his time at B&B, leaving behind both fans and critics. To his fans, he was bright, creative, unorthodox and fun to be around. To his critics, he was arrogant, irresponsible, unorthodox and aggravating to be around. Howard happened to be a fan, so Jerry was coming to the party.*

*When he arrived we started slowly and I had little trouble understanding the arrogance label. While he knew perfectly well who I was, his first comment to me alluded to the impossible task faced by the poor soul who had to "fill his shoes!" I uttered some lame response as the room rang with laughter. "Just kidding," he allowed, once his entrance had been deemed successful. He moved easily from person to person, eliciting more laughter at each stop. I noted that even Jerry's detractors sought his attention and roared at his cutting humor. None were free from his barbs. Mine had merely been the opening salvo to working the room and making sure that everyone present was clear about exactly who he was. There are people who can't stand someone like Jerry. Once over my initial reaction, however, I was more bemused by the show he put on than anything else. It was one I would see again from a different perspective.*

*A while later, sitting with Howard and chatting about why he had taken the job at Lever, Jerry plopped down on a chair to join us. He was a bit worn out from all the energy he'd expended.*

*"Show over Jerry?" Howard asked.*

*"What are you talking about Howard?" Jerry responded a bit testily.*

*"Apologize to Rob for that crappy comment you made when you walked in. In fact, he hasn't had any problem filling your shoes at all, especially since you stopped filling them yourself a long time before you left here. Though I must say that you are so talented it was worth having you, even*

*if you were cheating both us and yourself. No Jerry, we've done just fine. By the way, are you still cheating yourself?"*

*I was somewhat stunned. What do you say? Howard had just, quietly, leveled Jerry at the knees. It was obvious that Howard had been deeply disappointed by Jerry's actions and was taking this opportunity to let him have it while he had the chance.*

*"Howard," I said. "Whatever your beef may be with Jerry, he's here to honor you at what is, by the way Howard, a party for you! Get it? A party. So lighten up and let's get on with the fun. Okay?"*

*Things soon got back on track, and I kicked off the roast on Howard. Several of those present made comments about their experience with him and what he'd meant to their life and career. The most poignant of these comments was offered by Jerry, who spoke last. There were few dry eyes when he finished, followed by lots of hugging and best wishes offered before everyone went their way.*

*Several days later, the phone rang in my office. It was Jerry, apologizing and asking if I'd have lunch with him. It was the beginning of a strange, yet wonderful friendship that lasted for many years, and during which I learned a great deal about the normalcy of human frailty and imperfection, especially my own. I also had a lot of fun and made some progress toward growing into the person I am today.*

*The cheating that Howard was referring to related to Jerry's descent into self-destructive behavior including alcohol abuse. It was as if he had to see just how outrageous he could be and still be accepted. He had to challenge everyone's precept of what was acceptable. Underneath it all, was a profound lack of self-esteem that he had just begun sorting out at the time that we met.*

*Jerry had been earning a relatively high salary for some time. In spite of this, he lived in a studio apartment in Greenwich Village, that could only be described as rank squalor. I had occasion to visit him there once and was shocked by what I encountered when I entered. The place was covered with piles of clothes, towels, sheets, and whatnot everywhere, all* over the place. I'm not talking about neat piles. I'm talking about heaps of dirty, wrinkled stuff.

Even that, however, did not prepare me for what greeted me when I had to use the bathroom. Having run out of room to stack dirty dishes, pans, partially eaten containers of Chinese food and the like, Jerry had completely filled the bathtub and littered the floor with such things. When I turned on the light, an army of cockroaches scurried for cover and a shudder of disgust ran through me. I gasped, shocked all the more because of his seeming indifference to the filth he was living in. I quickly shut the bathroom door and explained that I would wait for him at a restaurant down the street. He actually expressed dismay at my squeamishness.

Another example of Jerry's state was illustrated by a meeting we both attended. It was a very hot day and the air conditioning had gone off. When Jerry spotted me and walked over to say hello, I couldn't help but notice that he was perspiring profusely. I had already taken my jacket off and suggested that he do the same.

"I can't, " he said.

"Why?" I asked.

He explained that he had been out late and had consumed too much alcohol the night before. As a result, he'd been so hung over that he'd had to rush to make the meeting. He'd only had a chance to iron the collar and cuffs of his shirt. The rest was a mess of wrinkles, not to mention already soaked. I tried not to but I had to laugh.

"What's so funny?" he said, clearly not appreciating my mirth.

"Well Jerry, it's really not funny, so I'm sorry I laughed. But how does someone who is obviously as smart and accomplished in his field as you are, be so out of control? You live like you're one step from being a derelict in the gutter. What gives?"

My comment made him furious. His face turned bright red and he huffed at me. "You little shit! Who do you think you are to talk to me like that? You can't carry my briefcase, nonetheless fill my shoes." With that, he was gone.

*It was some time before I heard from Jerry again. He called to invite me to see the new apartment he'd just taken. Afterwards, he told me that he had started seeing a therapist in order to get a handle on why his life was running amuck, and that he'd made certain decisions. Foremost of these was that he was going to get his master's degree in psychology and counseling.*

*Furthermore, he intended to devote his life to working with people who had problems and needed help getting back on track. His current work, he said, was just not fulfilling. He felt he had been wasting his intelligence. He wanted to challenge himself for the dual purpose of getting a handle on himself and his own life as well as helping others to experience more fulfillment in theirs. He was uniquely qualified to do this, he reasoned, since as I had so unpleasantly pointed out, he himself had experienced such personal lows.*

*His plan was to combine work and school. His company had agreed to let him set his own hours, as long as he delivered the creative ideas necessary. They were quite relieved and receptive when he approached them with the idea, since they too had become alarmed by his lapses. A sober, productive and happy part-time Jerry could not possibly be worse than the recent full-time model.*

*It took several years for Jerry to earn his degree. Aside from the academics, he had to work in various city clinics, counseling people while under supervision himself. Every now and then I'd see him and be reminded of what a miracle was occurring. At one point, Jerry started seeing patients privately and in groups. He then went on to earn his Ph.D. in psychology. Fast forward to today, Jerry has a thriving private practice, two beautiful homes, a loving and long-standing marriage and many people who are grateful to have him in their life – Certainly, including me!*

# THE MYSTERY

Sound reasoning would dictate that the early and continuing education of all people would include the natural laws of nature that effect human experience, and the relationship of a person's thoughts, words, and actions to the conditions of that individual's life.

This, in fact, has not been the case, with the result that *other people or circumstances* are often mistakenly thought of as the cause for one's woes. Most people go through life blaming luck, fate, their parents, education, their spouse, their children, their biorythms, the weather, the economy, the stars, and a host of other forces for their situation in life, rather than understanding that the person in the mirror and that person alone is most likely the cause of where they find themselves.

One of life's mysteries is why most people have such difficulty making this connection for themselves, particularly when it is so often apparent in others. That is, however, the way it is, and each individual is charged with learning this truth for themselves and applying it to their own lives.

As adults, if we read a newspaper story about someone who killed their spouse or children being convicted for murder and sentenced to life imprisonment, we most likely would think, *Of course, that person should be put away for good.* Likewise, nobody would question the validity of the punishments received by participants of various government and corporate corruption cases.

We don't seem to have a hard time grasping that life has simply served up to those people exactly what they deserved. In these very blatant examples we can clearly understand the relationship between the actions those people took and the subsequent impact on the conditions of their lives.

*The utterly amazing fact is that even with so many obvious examples all around, that prove conclusively that the saying, what goes around, comes around is true, people still participate in unbelievably self-destructive actions.*

One example from recent memory was the revelation that New York City inspectors were shaking down restaurant owners for bribes, in exchange for not reporting of health-code infractions. This came on the heels of numerous investigations and convictions of other city officials on charges of gross misconduct and fraud in carrying out their public duty.

With the newspapers and televisions full of discourse on these events, the restaurant inspectors in question went right on with their villainous activities as though they existed in a different universe. How could it be? You'd think they would quit, or at least take a low profile for a while. But no, they blithely went along apparently believing that only the other guys get caught.

This just points out what a hurdle of understanding and self-honesty is needed to get control of things. It begins with knowing that if one finds oneself in an unpleasant situation and wonders how they arrived there, the best place to turn for the answer is in that mirror.

Consider the following:

- A man, married with two children, is locked out of his house and forbidden by law to contact his wife or see his children except under supervision, following a violent outburst of temper.

- A manufacturing supervisor loses his job due to poor job performance and constant complaining.

- A young man who has consistently been in the center of trouble is told he may not return to the school he's attended due to poor academic and behavioral performance.

- What are the chances that these people will look in the mirror for the fairly obvious explanation of their troubles? If, through some stroke of luck, the light goes on, the bell goes ding-a-ling and there is a flickering of understanding, that is the first step.

- *If* the man says, "Gee, I guess I'm not allowed to indulge my temper like that if I want to have a meaningful relationship or any relationship at all with my wife and children."

- *If* the supervisor says, "Wow, I really messed this job up. I better make a serious assessment of my attitude and work ethic if I want someone to pay me a good salary so I can support my family."

- *If* the boy thinks, "Oh, so I really do have to respect the rules, do my homework and study if I want to stay in school."

*If these people knew that they were operating under a specific law every bit as exact as, "one plus one equals two," it would most likely, hopefully, be much easier for them to make this leap of understanding, and actually change their behavior accordingly.*

# THE R.D. CHRONICLES

*Yes indeed, R.D. is me. Of course, I have a much easier time pointing out brilliant observations about almost anyone other than myself. However, since the aforementioned begins to get to the crux of how all this going around and coming around works, I must face the music myself, as my own examples demand equal exposure.*

*Here's the thing. After spending years denying my personal responsibility for whatever was wrong with my life, it is quite discomforting to spell out my very own demons. It is tantamount to out-and-out admission of malfunction. It could open the floodgates of self-examination, which is so much easier to demand of someone else...*

# R.D. Story Number One (Teeth)

*I have a vivid memory of one particular summer which turned out to be the worst on record in this particular life. I was ten or eleven years old and was consuming prodigious quantities of candy on a daily basis. This had not gone totally unnoticed and I had been warned repeatedly by the appropriate hobgoblins about the evils of eating too many sweets.*

*What ten or eleven year old, however, really believes any of that bunk. Just parental nonsense. It was not, after all, as if I was depending on anyone to pay for my indulgence. On the contrary, between my two newspaper routes and my lawn cutting and watering business, I had plenty of cash flow to fund my appetite for such classics as Neccos, Dots and Chocolate Babies, not to mention my still favorites, Mounds Bars and Hershey Crunch. More importantly, who knew my teeth better than me?*

*I can still remember coming home after delivering my papers that fateful day, my mother waiting at the front door. "Come quickly," she said. "Dr. Elster wants us to come over to his office right away." Can you imagine the bad luck of having your dentist live right next door? Such was my misfortune. "Something about the X-rays he did of your mouth, at your check-up last week," she said.*

*"Thanks for coming right over," he told her. "I just finished developing these and am very concerned. If what they show is correct, we have a serious problem. I wanted to take a look for myself as soon as possible."*

*"What are you talking about?" she said. "What kind of a problem? You're scaring me."*

*"Cavities," he answered. "Lots and lots of cavities. I have never, in my career, seen so many cavities in one child's mouth at one time. If these X-rays are right, we're talking about more than twenty cavities, and some of them look like doozies."*

Let me just mention here, that I had really been looking forward to this summer. It had been a bear of a fourth grade year. Dates, dates and more dates to remember. Explorers, conquerors, wars, treaties, you name it. It was also a year of serious grammar, conjugating sentences and the like. Totally depressing. Summer, ah summer. A time of no school and relative freedom. What could be more wonderful than that?

Not the look on my mother's face, that's for sure. She had gasped at Dr. Elster's words and was an ashen color as she awaited the verdict. I was never sure if it was fear for her son or pure unadulterated rage that caused the pallor, but I immediately began to get the sense that this latest development was definitely not a good thing.

To make matters worse, Dr. Elster's pokes here and there with that pointed silver thing in my mouth were killing me. "Oh, hurts does it?" he'd say, grinding it in a bit harder. "How about over here?"

"Arrgghh," I'd reply with a wince.

"Oh really," he'd respond.

"Mrs. Davis," he finally said to my mom. "This is unbelievable. I just hope we don't have a situation here where we actually lose some teeth, though I can't rule that out. We have to get started on this right away. It may take two or three appointments a week to get all of these filled by the end of the summer, but the main question is, what in the world has this boy been eating?"

I could go into the details of the conversation (did I say conversation?) I had with my parents that night, or the pleasure of the thrice weekly visits I had with Dr. Elster that summer, but why do that to you? If I try – and it doesn't take much – I can still hear the sound of that drill in my head and feel its grinding vibration. Even worse, I never did get used to the look and feel of the needle when he administered the Novocain. The resulting numbness seemed to last forever, but it was definitely preferable to the agony without it.

But enough said about that. The worst part was – can you guess? What? You don't know? You don't get it? That's right! I had to give up my Mounds bars and Nestle Crunch. I had to kiss goodbye my Chocolate Babies and Dots. Just looking at them set off the sound of that drill in my head.

One Sunday afternoon following our family dinner, my father was passing around pieces of a delicious-looking cake he'd just made. It was steaming warm and gooey and smelled great. "No thanks," I said when it came to my turn.

# R.D. Story Number Two (Failure)

*If I had to choose a personal example of failure or disappointment in myself, I'd have to say it was the way I handled my first marriage and the subsequent effect on my first child, Nan. I am very grateful that in spite of all that transpired over the years, she remains an important presence in my life. Moreover, her two sons Bryan and Joshua and Bryan's son, Jameson are absolute treasures!*

*This is not to say that the marriage should have or could have lasted any longer than the six years it did. Had I been more mature, however. Had I been less selfish. Might I have been able to do a better job of protecting her from the ravages of the war that her mother and I engaged in? Wudda, cudda, shudda. Well, I wasn't and didn't. As a result, all the participants suffered, but none so more than Nan.*

*She was born on March 8, 1965, three months before my twentieth birth-day. My mother drove to our upstate college town apartment from Long Island, where I had grown up. She came to be present at the hospital and to help out for a few days, as I was taking six courses that semester and had four exams the day Nan was born.*

*Nan's mother and I had discovered that she was pregnant during the summer after my freshman year. We were gripped by panic initially, but ultimately decided to get married, stick together and have our child. At the time, there was really not all that much in the way of choice. Though the world would change dramatically in the next ten years, 1965 was still much the way it had always been. And unlike today, appearances mattered a lot. Unless you were really "far out," you just did not live together unless you were married. Having a baby absolutely required getting married and at our socio-economic level, getting an abortion was simply not an option.*

*Regardless, once I saw Nan, I was blown away by the wonderment of it all. If I'd had any doubts before then, they vanished in that moment. I was in love with mother and child and determined to be the best husband and father I could.*

*When Nan arrived on the scene, I was still working on finishing my sophomore year of college. Nan's mom had one more semester to go before she could graduate and begin the teaching job she'd been offered for the fall. These circumstances, plus the fact that we had no money, were merely incidental conditions to a much larger story. The important thing was that we were starting to carve out our own space in the world. Far from feeling that I was missing something, or too young for such a responsibility, I took it as a challenge to prove that I could handle it. I was convinced that we'd find a way.*

*On a certain level, we did. Between helpful mothers, friends and ourselves, we somehow got through Nan's first precious months. Her mom successfully completed her courses and graduated. In the fall, she began teaching. I found part-time jobs and loaded up on courses so I could graduate as soon as possible. Grades suffered, but eventually I made it too. My first job upon graduation was to teach a sixth grade class at the Oak Grove School in Wappingers Falls, New York. It was the fall of 1966. I had graduated in just under three action packed years.*

*There we were, two kids in their early twenties with a baby, full-time jobs, college loans, car loans, baby-sitting expenses, rent, etc. Everything was so serious and there was zero relief, except that is, for the joy that Nan brought to us each day. Unfortunately, my skills at handling the conflicts of interpersonal relationships were deficient. We had been so deeply into simple survival, just putting one foot in front of the other, that the romance category had been pretty well squashed. Before long, everything seemed to be about issues of life and whose will would prevail.*

*We stayed together for another three years, struggling with life and each other. Basically, I blamed her for just about everything. She was far more accepting of me than vice versa. It all had to be my way or the highway. On reflection, I could have handled things much better than I did. But every issue seemed to me one matter of life and death, as though if I did not triumph, I would somehow disappear.*

*It would be some time before I had the benefit of psychological counseling and could begin to understand my contribution to the break-up of the marriage. Therapy, at the time, was not something I would have dreamed of. At the time, it would have meant that I was weak, crazy or both. Not acceptable. How differently society would judge such matters in just a few years. Too late for me, however, to deal with the damaged state I was apparently in then.*

*When we split, it was very rough on Nan. Her mother brimmed with anger toward me. Once she determined that we were definitely through, she turned her full fury towards destroying my relationship with Nan. It would not be possible to measure the extent of the damage wrought unto Nan by the split of her parents and the subsequent wars waged for her affection.*

*My entire life and Nan's have been colored by this situation. Thankfully, we have both found our measures of peace. Even though I have been blessed to move on, I am forever mindful of the potential result of thoughtless expressions of ego, self-centered control and manipulation. Having said that, I am far from free of the urges to employ them.*

*The point is, I can't very well persist in blaming Nan's mother for causing me unhappiness when I keep telling everyone else to look in the mirror. I regret that I was not better equipped to handle all that needed to be dealt with as a younger parent. But I am committed to continuing to strive toward self-revealing scrutiny and self-inflicted growth in order to avoid future such blunders.*

# R.D. Story Number Three (Marathon)

*There is no getting around the fact that there is a certain degree of lunacy involved in the preparation and running of an official, 26.2 mile marathon. While I have repeatedly denied the relevance of that observation to myself personally, what can one say after completing fourteen of them, except to acknowledge that, "If the shoe fits..." For the uninitiated, however, it is important to point out that there are redeeming qualities to this seemingly crazed activity, and as soon as I can think of one, I will gladly point it out!*

*Regardless, in the summer of 1991, I decided to try for the Holy Grail for most marathon runners, qualifying for the Boston Marathon, clearly the granddaddy and most prestigious marathon in the world. It is distinguished by the tradition of the race, the beauty of the course, the dreaded three tier Heartbreak Hill, and the spirit of the crowds lining it from beginning to end. Also, unlike every other marathon which can be entered by anyone having the nerve and who completes the application process, to run in Boston one needs to have completed an officially sanctioned marathon during the previous calendar year, in an age group qualifying time.*

*"So what?" you might say. "What's the big deal?" Well, the big deal is that those qualifying times are challenging, to say the least. Most people who run a marathon, do so with the hope of breaking four hours. To qualify for Boston, however, a man of 50 has to break three hours and twenty-five minutes. A man of 25 or less needs to break three hours. In the case of the former, that means averaging faster than 8 minute miles for the entire 26.2 miles. That is really moving. In 1991, at the age of 46 years old, my qualifying time to allow me the privilege of running the Boston Marathon was three hours twenty-five minutes.*

*To put it in perspective, up to this time I had run six marathons, with times ranging from 3:25:21 (run in the '89 New York Marathon) to 4:11:09 (my* first run in the '87). Since I had come so close in my '89 effort, I felt that I could achieve my goal if I had the right plan and stuck with it. In '89 I had faltered in the last two miles with a shooting pain in my gut. What had appeared at mile 24 to be a sure thing, slipped away as I struggled to the finish line. My subsequent 1990 effort produced a lackluster 3:46 result.

The question now was, could I inspire myself with the dedication of purpose needed to discipline and drive myself over the next few months, to do the things required? This meant eliminating unproductive distractions, getting proper diet and rest, and putting in the miles to achieve my goal. It would mean turning up the intensity notch and putting myself in the position to attack those last two miles rather than be humbled by them. I had to ask myself if that is what I really wanted. My answer was yes!

Once having made that decision, the first step was to formulate, "The Plan." I had learned, through painful experience, the price of not having a plan, or of having one that was inadequate for the goals I wished to achieve. I had also been taught in the most effective way the truth of the old axiom that, "There is many a slip twixt the cup and the lip," referring in this instance to the wide gap that can exist between having a plan and executing that plan.

I was very lucky at the time in that I had two terrific running buddies. Both were fun and competitive to run with and both embraced the idea of helping me get ready for my quest. I'd been running with Chip on the weekend mornings since the winter of '84. We'd typically meet at 6:30 A.M. on Saturday and Sunday mornings, run for between one and three hours, and be back and showered by the time the day was starting for everyone else. My other running pal, Steve, and I ran together during the week in the city. Sometimes at lunch, other times at the end of the day, we'd meet at a midtown health club, change and go out for a loop of Central Park. It was about eight miles to and from the club. It was a rare week that didn't include at least two runs. More often, it was three or four.

Chip is a powerful and relentless pounder. He can go on and on but his pace is not of the greyhound variety. This suited me fine for our long weekend runs. We'd mosey along and chat about everything going on in life and end up spent, and having covered quite a few miles. Steve, on the other hand, ran marathons in the early '80's and completed three of them under three hours (less than a seven minute mile pace). Though he was no longer running marathons, he was still a heck of a runner, and our jaunts in the park were anything but leisurely.

My plan was to run three times during the week with Steve, preferably Tuesday, Wednesday and Thursday, leaving Monday and Friday for rest days. Saturday would be my long run day and Sunday would be hill day. My thinking was that after three days in a row with Steve, I should give my body one day of rest before my long run, which would be increased a couple of miles each week until I was in the 20-22 mile range. I hoped to complete at least three training runs at that 20 plus mile length before the 1991 New York Marathon, scheduled for the first Sunday in November.

The Steve part of the plan was simple. At this point, our routine was fairly set. We'd meet at a health club on East 52$^{nd}$, change into our running stuff and hit the road. We'd head up Park Avenue to 60$^{th}$ Street, hang a left and enter Central Park across from the Plaza. Six miles later, panting and soaked, we'd head back to the shower. In between, we'd battle the hills, race the flats and never, ever, if possible, let anyone pass us by. In other words, there was not much I could do to improve on that part of my regimen. It was already about as rigorous as I could stand.

A word about the hill training portion of the program. In '89, Chip and I had discovered "hill workouts." There was a street not far from where we lived in Greenwich, Connecticut called North Maple. Just past the Greenwich Academy, a school my girls attended, the street plunged downward in a steep pitch. At the bottom it proceeded around a curve and then began to ascend. The climb to the back entrance of Deer Park was not as steep, but quite a bit longer. All in all, it was almost exactly a half-mile from peak to peak. We considered one rep to constitute a complete loop, down and up, then back down and up to where we began, or one mile. Every Sunday possible in our training that year, we'd throw in a "hill" day, completing as many as 10 to 12 reps in a single workout.

The way it worked was that we'd cruise down the hill and around the curve, then pick up the pace as we hit the hill. Arms pumping, legs churning and lungs bursting, we'd dig it out, side by side, until finally, we'd reach the top gasping for air. Then we'd turn around and head back down the hill, hoping to recover by the time we hit the other hill back up. It was a brutal work-out that left our legs feeling wobbly and the rest of us exhausted, but it was a tremendous strength builder. I think it's what helped me do so well that year and I determined to make it a more regular part of my training regimen this time.

So "The Plan" was set. Three days a week with Steve, a long run on Saturday and a hill workout on Sunday. My weekly mileage would increase as my Saturday runs lengthened and the number of reps in my hill workouts increased.

Then I decided to throw in an extra ingredient. Three weeks prior to New York, the Marine Corps Marathon was scheduled in Washington, D.C. I decided that I would enter it and approach it as just another training run. I wouldn't be concerned about time and if necessary, I'd drop out at twenty miles so I didn't hurt my chances in New York. According to my training calendar, I would already have run two twenty milers by then anyway, so I didn't see why it should be a problem.

Many people run marathons after just one 16-18 mile practice run. I had learned from experience, however, that while one might be able to finish a marathon on that regimen, the chances of doing it painlessly, or in a great time, were not very good. I felt that I'd be ready to run the Marine Corps and that it would make me stronger for New York, three weeks later.

Now came the hard part. The actual doing of the work, day in and day out. Keeping my attention on the goal. It's amazing, once you set your mind on doing something, how many things come up to throw you off course. I had plenty. There were job reasons to skip, family reasons to skip, not to mention my own lethargy. There were late Friday and Saturday nights which made getting out for my early weekend runs painful. Then there were those dreaded hills, on the day following my long run.

Who had thought up that dumb idea? My legs felt so dead when I started out on some of those Sunday mornings that I wondered how I'd complete even one rep. But something would happen. Once I got myself out the door and started sucking in the fresh morning air, and the blood started circulating in my legs, I'd forget the pain and get into my groove. There were even a few days when Chip was gone and I was on my own to churn out the reps. Six, eight, ten, one more... now eleven, one more... now twelve.

By early October I could feel the power building in my legs. The problem I was having was getting loose. Just walking around I could feel tightness in my hamstrings. I stretched every moment I could, fearful that something would pop and thwart the plan. Several people told me I was nuts to run Marine Corps so close to New York. They said that I'd never recover in time and end up wasting both races. Well, I thought, qualifying for the Boston Marathon was my goal, not theirs. I'd have to pursue it according to my plan, not theirs. Maybe they knew themselves, but I was the one who knew me best, and I was the one who would have to live with the results, whether I achieved my goal or not.

As I stood on the starting line of the Marine Corps Marathon that October day, I was struck by the beauty of the surroundings, the cracker jack efficiency and organization of the event, and the perfection of the day. It was exactly 50 degrees and overcast as the crowd awaited the starting guns retort, just the right temperature for me.

I had flown down the previous afternoon, checked into a nearby hotel, had my obligatory pasta dinner and hit the sack. On my flight there was a guy from Stamford, Connecticut. He was running his fiftieth marathon, and he regaled me with war stories about his various experiences for the entire flight. Both Steve and Chip had called me with their encouragement. Steve told me to go out hard and try to sustain it for as long as possible. Chip gave me his trademark advice, "Start slow, and taper off."

I thanked them both and assured each of them that I'd follow their instructions faithfully. Until the gun went off that is. For the truth is that once it does, nothing anyone has said means a thing. You are truly on your own in a way that only a marathoner can understand. It's you and your body *and the road. If you're ready, your body and you have a great time and the road is your friend sharing the trip. If not ...ouch!*

*The gun went off at 10:00 A.M. There was a nip in the air and the sky was slightly overcast. The crowd of twelve thousand runners, was in high spirits as it began to surge forward on a journey that would cover 26.2 miles. The winner would finish in two hours and twelve minutes, while some would still be straggling in after six hours. As for me, I was just out for a nice run.*

*Keeping to my plan, I started easy and just cruised. The Marines, strategically stationed along the course, were great. They shouted encouragement, handed out water at intervals and kept the crowds along the way orderly and enthused. After a couple of miles, I began to warm up. I shed my expendable hat, gloves and sweatshirt, knowing that I'd left a bag of warm sweats at the finish line to change into.*

*I had passed the five mile marker at about an eight minute, thirty second per mile pace, much slower than I'd need to qualify, but fine for this Sunday jaunt. Then, just shy of eight miles, something totally unexpected happened. It was the kind of serendipitous event that can only happen when you are out there doing your thing and are prepared to take advantage of it. If you're not, it just zips on by and you're not quite sure what happened or what you might have missed. If you're ready, however, you find out. You grab hold and go for the ride. In this case, it was quite a ride indeed.*

*His name was Jacque and he was in the process of passing me, when for some reason, he turned his head toward me and said a cheerful, "Hello." I said, "Hi, where are you from?" It turns out he could barely speak English, but I was able to learn that he and his wife lived in France and were visiting Washington so he could run the marathon. He'd also be running in New York three weeks later. This was his tenth marathon. When I asked him his name, he looked at me quizzically, not understanding, so I pointed at myself and said, "Me ...Rob, me ...Rob." He got it, laughed and pointed at himself saying, "Me ...Jacque, me ...Jacque." Simple minded as that was, we got a good laugh out of it and instantly bonded.*

We just sort of started running together. Our strides locked into each other and the pace picked up dramatically. For the next twelve miles, we surged past runner after runner. At water stops, we'd alternately grab cups for each other. As we approached clumps of runners, we'd strategize with hand signals how best to pass them. It was so much fun that the miles just ticked off and before I knew it, we'd had flown past the twenty mile mark. It was great. Then, suddenly, with the same bolt that brought it to me, it was gone. Jacque poked me, shrugged and pointed to the side of the road. "Go Rob, go," he said. Before I could protest, he was headed for the bushes alongside the road to relieve himself. It was the last I saw of him.

So there I was just approaching 21 miles and on my own. I'd been so into the fun of running with Jacque that I hadn't really been aware of the time. But as I went past the clock at twenty-one miles, the thought struck me that wow, I was actually within shouting distance of a 3:25 finish. I calculated that I had traversed the first 21 miles at an average of seven minutes, fifty seconds per mile. If I could do the last 5.2 miles slightly faster at a 7:40 pace, I might have a chance.

The thought, though, was crazy! Nobody ran the last five miles of a marathon faster than the first 21. It was the opposite. Oh, but I was so close, I thought. If only Jacque were still with me, maybe. Then I thought of his "Go Rob, go!" I just said to myself, "Come on, man. Bear down. Remember the hills. Each mile is just one more hill. Do it!"

The finish line of the Marine Corps Marathon begins at the bottom of a short, but what I remember as fairly steep, path up to a quarter mile track. The path and the track are packed with spectators yelling and screaming encouragement. I hit the path flying but the hill really drained me and I was gasping as I started around the track toward the finish. I was hurting, elated and desperate at the same time. There'd been no clocks for the last couple of miles and while I thought I was close, I just wasn't sure.

Around the track I went, digging down for whatever I had left. I kept expecting to see the finish line just around the bend, but the damned thing just kept going on and on. Then at last, there it was, about 120 yards *away. I looked up and could see the clock ticking away. People were screaming, "You've got it, you've got it. Dig it out, come on, dig it out."*

*I could barely believe my eyes. It read three hours, twenty-four minutes, twenty seconds. All I could think was, "Come on, legs, move." With all I had left I ran what was probably the slowest sprint of my life, but it was enough to get me under the line at three hours, twenty-four minutes, forty-three seconds. I did it! I had broken three hours, twenty-five minutes ...by seventeen seconds.*

*It's hard to describe what that moment was like. I let out a primal scream. I thrust both fists to the sky. I was so happy at that moment, I thought I would burst with joy. A Marine met me at the end of the chute. He put a medal around my neck and a runner's blanket around my shoulders.*

*"Great run," he said. "Congratulations."*

*"Thanks," I said. "Really, thanks."*

# R.D. Story Number Four (Hedge Funds Care/Help for Children)

*It was the Fall of 1998 and I was not a happy camper. In fact, I was feeling really bad about myself. During the summer I had fallen down on a commitment I'd made to a friend, to help him bring people out for a charitable event he was working on. I had all kinds of excuses for why I faded so badly. There had been kids issues, injury issues, work issues, all crap, but he was very nice about it. The event had been a great success in spite of me – and he was totally gracious – but I knew! I knew I had bailed on him, and the important issue it was for.*

*It was a Sunday evening in September and I was sitting at the desk in my home office with an article I had put aside to read in front of me. But mainly I was thinking bad thoughts about myself. Then I jumped from the frying pan into the fire. There on the bookshelf in staring at me was a book my daughter Genevieve had gotten me for my birthday, four months before, Timeless Wisdom, a Book of Quotes, and I hadn't so much as opened the cover. "God," I thought. "I am simply a bad person. Fell down on my friend. Couldn't even take the time to open the book from my daughter and glance through. What is wrong with me?"*

*Needing to change the subject to relieve the moment I looked at the article. It was about the demise of one of the largest and most highly respected hedge funds at that time, Long Term Capital Management (LTCM).*

*LTCM was one of the darlings of the hedge fund world, having generated consistently high returns for its first few years in business. The staff was blue chip, including two Nobel Prize winners plus a cadre of seasoned Wall Street pros, collaborating to develop their trading and execution strategies. The Firm's mystique grew as both strategies and trades were kept top secret, and Wall Street firms competed fiercely for their business.*

*So fierce in fact, that firms with strict criteria for doing business, including allowable levels of margin and capital requirements, began to abandon their own hard learned standards, offering previously unheard of terms on rates and leverage to LTCM, to capture their piece of the action. They were also required to keep their dealings with LTCM, including pricing and trades in strictest confidence. The result was that none of the investment banks who were financing LTCM's positions knew what the others were doing, or had the big picture of LTCM's over-all risk exposure.*

*The LTCM partners though, obviously believed their own rhetoric. They took all the capital they could get the Wall Street firms to lend them, bending every rule of borrowing/leverage in the book and building a mountain of assets on what became, relatively speaking, a very small capital base.*

*Then suddenly, in the blink of an eye those secret strategies stopped working. Their positions all started going against them at the same time. Because of their enormous leverage they rapidly blew through their capital to the point where bankruptcy was almost at hand.*

*It would have been another story of "just desserts," were it not for the huge portfolio of securities that such a bankruptcy would have forced the market to absorb. So huge that it was feared many unsuspecting market participants would have been swiftly put out of business, and necessitating then Fed Chairman Alan Greenspan to get involved in working out a solution.*

*They did indeed work one out that saved a cataclysm from resulting. In the end it was the LTCM Partners who rightfully took the brunt in losing most of their equity in LTCM, in return for the capital that Greenspan coerced from the banks to buy time until the trades worked out. So in essence, the risk was mostly transferred, through Greenspan's action, to the foolish investment banks who had abrogated their own policies to chase the LTCM siren allure.*

*To those who actually understood what had happened, Alan Greenspan had swiftly analyzed the systemic risk of the situation, figured out the culprits, and acted swiftly and decisively to avert a crisis. Those who did not understand, thought it was some kind of a government bailout that benefitted only the big guys. Not true. If fact, the investment banks involved could have lost the total amount of capital they had to put up at Greenspan's insistence.*

*Eventually the trades in question worked out. The banks recovered their capital and then some. But that didn't help the LTCM partners, particularly the younger ones who had borrowed money to buy in during the previous couple of years. In a prime example of the two-edged sword of leverage, they lost everything and still had to repay their debt.*

*The two authors of the article I read that evening were academics who had no clue. Based on the vehemence of their comments, they did not seem to understand that LTCM was not at all representative of the hedge fund industry at large. Yet they blasted the entire industry as being just as risky as LTCM had turned out to be. Being on the custodial, prime brokerage side of the business, I knew that the vast majority of hedge fund managers approached leverage with caution. That's because in most cases the managers have all or most of their own invested capital in the fund they manage, and so "eat their own cooking."*

*As I read the article, I became agitated on behalf of the industry, both that the Professors would write such an article, and that the publication would run it. And it was in that moment that I was struck by the idea that would lead to the formation of Hedge Funds Care. It occurred to me that someone should use the article to bring the industry together for a good cause, to counteract the terrible publicity of the article at hand and others like it.*

*At about the same time, I again noticed the book from Genevieve. As I said it was now four months after my birthday and I hadn't so much as cracked it open. "Ok fool," I thought, open the darn book! Rather than start at the beginning, I open it to a random page. The first quote I read is one I had heard before:*

*"The road to hell is paved with good intentions!"*

*That gave me a little shiver down my spine as I thought about the friend I had let down. It was the kind you get when you know you've been caught dead to rights! My intention had been fine, but my follow-through was* terrible! It was not even a zero score. It was actually a zero minus even more. Then I saw the other half of that quote for the first time.

"The road to heaven is paved with good actions!"

That was like an arrow though my neck! Where were my actions on my friend's behalf? The actions I had promised. Without actions, my promise had been hollow and good for nothing!

Add to it the fact that I was just now reading this book? A gift from my child's! Bad, bad man! Then it got worse! I turned to another page, and another quote jumped out at me. It said:

"We're all alike in what we say. It's in what we do that we differ."

I was struck by the proverbial ton of bricks. "Come on man," my brain screamed. "You need to take some actions, and you need to do so now!" My brain continued; "So you think that someone should use the article to bring people together for a good cause, huh? Well fool...how about that person being you!"

It worked! The next morning I went to see my two bosses. I explained my, "reverse the bad publicity by raising money and doing something good" theory. I asked their blessing, for me to try pulling together a party of industry people I had met at conferences and in the course of doing business. It would be to raise money for the prevention and treatment of child abuse. "Picture it," I said:

"Hedge Funds Care" invites you to "The Open Your Heart To the Children Benefit"

They asked me what I was going to charge. I thought back to my friend's benefit and what he charged. I said, "$8,000 for a table of ten." They looked at each other and said in unison, "We'll take the first table!" And thus was Hedge Funds Care born. Of course, as some Granny once said,

"There's many a slip, 'twixt the cup and the lip!"

Which of course is quite true. The story of what unfolded over the next four months to make that first benefit party the raging success it was, is a tale unto itself and will be told. For the moment, suffice it to say that *over the intervening years up to the present, many thousands of children, in the cities and countries where there are now "Hedge Funds Care/Help For Children" branches (www.HFC.org), have received prevention training, and where damage has already been done, highly professional clinical treatment.*

*On another note, my friend, yes the one I let down, has attended many HFC events over the years. At one of our golf outings he said to me, "Geez! It just occurred to me that if you hadn't been upset with yourself back then, all this might never have happened!" Then with a big smile, "Damned good thing you screwed me over! I think I should take credit for all of this!" We had a good laugh which ended with my, "I agree!"*

# THE EPIDEMIC

The continual unfolding of events, and the revelation of subsequent results throughout the world, illustrates just how much of a challenge making correct choices can be. This is due, in large measure, to the widespread confusion that exists regarding *"how life really works."* Even the most imaginative writers of fiction would be hard pressed to dream up the unceasing scenarios of real life dramas, about people from every nook and stratum of life who mindlessly throw monkey wrenches into their own lives.

They are all individuals, who for some reason, have failed to learn or chosen to ignore, the fundamental principles of life. It is not, however, a problem of some particular socio-economic, political, racial, or any other designation of group. Rather, it cuts across them all. Moreover, the effect is felt not only by the individual themselves, but also by related family members, communities, companies and even countries.

There is one aspect of this story which is particularly unfathomable, yet equally of interest to note. Namely, how little effect this endless and continual disclosure of dire results from debased actions appears to have on subsequent offenders. One might conclude that there is little or no connection made until the hammer of consequences arrives between one's own two eyes. Even then, in many cases, the culprit rationalizes away the truth as bad luck, or some other bogeyman.

This tendency to look anyplace but in the mirror for the explanation of why one's life has gone this way or that, seems to be a common characteristic of the human condition. One could explore this conundrum endlessly and still not resolve it.

That it is the case, however, is irrefutable. Whatever the reason, the result is a natural barrier to understanding and personal growth. It is a barrier that each individual must find a way to overcome themselves, in their own manner and at their own pace, in order to progress meaningfully toward realizing their highest goals. In order to overcome this hurdle, however, one must first "see" that it exists.

The following describes occurrences I have seen unfold over past years that typify the aforementioned. While it may seem as if the insider trading scandals of the past decade are unique examples of how easy it is to miss the connection between one's thoughts, words and actions and what will eventually show up in one's life, check out the following. It begins with a story reported in the *New York Times* when Rudolph Guiliani was still the U.S. Attorney for the Southern District of New York.

> *In a sting operation that swept from Long Island to the Canadian border, 58 people, including 44 New York municipal officials, have been charged with taking bribes and kickbacks from an undercover FBI agent. Virtually no bribe offered by the agent, who posed as a salesman of steel products, was refused.*
>
> *"On 106 occasions, bribes were offered or discussed " said Guiliani, who was prosecuting the cases. "On 105 of those occasions, the public official involved accepted the bribe, and the other occasion he turned it down because he didn't think it was enough." That official, Mr. Guiliani added, was later arrested on charges of taking other bribes.*
>
> *Mr. Guiliani and Thomas L. Sheer, head of the FBI's New York office, said the investigation highlighted an endemic corruption problem that extended beyond New York City, which itself has been the focus of major corruption scandals in recent years. In all, criminal charges named officials in forty towns.*
>
> *"We believe we have surfaced a deeply rooted system of corruption that rots the core of municipal government," Mr. Sheer said. "It is a way of life, a practice established over the years."*

From the point of view of this treatment, it is noteworthy that many of those involved were citizens of good standing in their communities, selected to fulfill the public trust in responsible positions. They represent normal, everyday people with homes, kids in school, aging parents, a family dog, and normal pressures and bills to pay. Somehow, though, they accepted in themselves as standard operating procedure, behavior that is totally unacceptable.

*They most likely failed to grasp the causal connection between their thoughts, words and actions and the resulting impact on their lives and the lives of those closest to them, the very ones they most want to protect!*

Due to this lack of understanding about *how life really works,* they created circumstances which now affect them in a very real way. They probably didn't think of themselves as crooks. They probably participated in joking about others who had fallen in various scandals, never considering themselves at the same risk or putting themselves in the same nefarious category.

A similarly mind-boggling story was reported by a Connecticut newspaper titled, "80 Fugitives Are Snared With Phony Mail." The article explained:

> *Police have rounded up 80 fugitives using a sting operation. The suspects were asked to pick up packages at a certain store. Hidden cameras in the store kept them under surveillance. They were greeted by an undercover officer posing as an employee who asked them to produce identification. Then the suspects, all of whom had failed to show up for scheduled court appearances, were arrested. The charges were for offenses related to drugs, larceny, robbery and motor vehicle violations.*

Who knows what might have gone through the minds of these individuals during the time that they knew they were evading the law. Some may have been sick with worry. Others may have had no concern or guilt at all. They may have believed that they were clever enough to avoid capture even though they had already been identified as a culprit.

Whatever may have been the case, the truth is that there was a mechanism set in motion by their actions, that was working away on bringing them to justice, but which they were seemingly unaware of. The day they walked into that store, however, they were rudely awakened to its existence.

"Irrelevant," one might say. " The individuals involved in these stories were obviously just plain stupid. No intelligent person would be such an idiot to do these things, much less get caught."

So it would seem. Further examination of the facts, however, reveals a far different story. To illustrate the endemic nature of the issue, the following is a selective chronicle of events which took place in the year 1995. They all involved prominent, intelligent and accomplished people, yet are all examples of how these individuals failed to grasp the causal connection between their thoughts, words and actions, and the resulting circumstances and conditions of their lives. The parallels to the scandals of post 2008 are stunning! Consider...

Reported in *USA Today* on June 23, 1995:

### *Headline – Charity Embezzler Gets 7-Year Term*

*William Aramony, the high-living ex-chief of United Way, was sentenced to seven years in prison Thursday for looting the coffers of the nation's largest charity network. Aramony's lawyer asked for leniency saying his client, 68, suffers from a degenerative brain disease and other medical problems. But U.S. District Judge Claude Hilton gave Aramony all but one of the eight years he faced under federal sentencing guidelines. "This is a tough, hard sentence that certainly sends a message to anyone responsible for stewardship of charitable accounts," said Assistant U. S. Attorney Randy Bellows.*

*Aramony headed the United Way for 22 years before allegations of financial impropriety forced him to resign in 1992. During the trial, prosecutors portrayed Aramony as a corrupt womanizer who spent hundreds of thousands of dollars of the charity's money to finance flings with young women and trips to Egypt, London, Paris and Las Vegas. Bellows put the final tally in the amount Aramony defrauded United Way at $1.2 million.*

On April 28 and June 29, 1995, the *Wall Street Journal* contained the three following stories. They were extraordinary in that they all involved people who were not only in positions of trust, but who also knew from firsthand experience the utter foolishness of the very activities in which they engaged.

### Headline – *Citron Pleads Guilty in Probe of Orange County Loss*

*Former Orange County Treasurer, Robert L. Citron, responsible for the biggest municipal bankruptcy ever, pleaded guilty to six felony charges of misleading investors and misrepresenting interest earnings from the county's doomed investment fund. Under a surprise plea, the county's 69-year old deposed top financial officer admitted making false entries and misappropriating public funds.*

*Under Mr. Citron's watch, the county's $7.4 billion investment portfolio was ravaged by $1.7 billion in losses at the end of last year, prompting massive layoffs of county workers and threatening defaults on county bonds. Mr. Citron faced up to 14 years in prison, but only spent one year behind bars. Adding to the tale, Merrill Lynch was accused of participating in the fraud and settled for a fine of $400 millon.*

\* \* \* \* \*

### Headline – *Former Attorney At Cravath Admits To SEC Charges*

*A former Cravath, Swaine & Moore attorney and his brother pleaded guilty to insider-trading charges in transactions involving several of the law firms' clients. Richard Woodward, who worked in Cravath's corporate-finance department as a senior associate, admitted that he gave his brother, John Woodward, a real-estate company employee, confidential information about 12 business deals between May 1990 and March 1995.*

*The 34 year-old lawyer and his brother, who is 35, each pleaded guilty to one criminal count of conspiracy to violate securities law. Total illegal profits of $933,000 were allegedly made by people* who traded on the inside information. Mr. Woodward was fired from Cravath in March for refusing to cooperate with the law firm's inquiry into suspicious trading by his brother. The National Association of Securities Dealers had notified Cravath in January that it was looking into the unusual trading.

* * * * *

### Headline - Hubbell Receives 21-Month Term For Bilking Firm

*Webster Hubbell, the former associate attorney general who is a key figure in the Whitewater investigation, was sentenced to 21 months in prison for bilking his law firm and some of its clients. Mr. Hubbell pleaded guilty last December to defrauding the Rose Law Firm, and to a lesser degree its clients, out of $482,410. He also admitted owing $143,747 in back taxes as a result of his fraud.*

*"Better than anyone, I know the severity of my actions and their tremendous consequences on others, "Mr. Hubbell told U. S. District Judge George Howard Jr., at his sentencing yesterday. "I simply became overwhelmed and was unable at that time to face up to my failures .... I was simply wrong." Mr. Hubbell also was sentenced to three years' probation and community service. He will be required to make $135,000 restitution.*

In a case that foretold the Harvey Weinstein cataclysm, on September 8, 1995, the *Wall Street Journal* and the *New York Times* carried headlines and extensive stories about Robert Packwood's resignation from the U.S. Senate.

### Headline - Packwood Resigns Senate Seat After Panel Details Evidence

*Excerpts:*

*The Senate Ethics Committee's 10,145 page compilation of evidence that led to Bob Packwood's resignation today paints a portrait of a senior Senator who altered evidence he thought might be incriminating, repeatedly tried to take advantage of women dependent on him for jobs and pressured lobbyists to provide consulting fees for his wife. "These were not merely stolen kisses as Senator Packwood has claimed," Senator McConnell, Chairman of the Ethics Committee said in describing Mr. Packwood's "physical coercion" of women. "There was a habitual pattern of aggressive, blatantly sexual advances, mostly directed at members of his own staff or others whose livelihoods were connected in some way to his power and authority as a Senator."*

*This was the culmination of a push by a strange and ultimately overpowering amalgam of women's organizations. At its nucleus were 17 women, most of whom had worked for or dealt with the five-term Republican in the 1970's and 1980's, who came forward with allegations of unwanted sexual advances shortly after his 1992 reelection. Then, in a surprising crescendo this week, the Senate swung into action and Senator Packwood was out.*

Reported in the *Wall Street Journal* on September 22, 1995:

### *Headline - <u>Lawyer Admits He Laundered Drug Money</u>*

*A Manhattan lawyer pleaded guilty yesterday to taking part in what officials called one of the largest money-laundering operations ever uncovered in New York City, a ring responsible for hiding more than $19 million in drug profits for the Cali cocaine cartel. The lawyer, Harvey Weinig, pleaded guilty in Federal Court in Manhattan to one count of conspiracy to commit money-laundering. Of the 14 people charged in the case, all but one have pleaded guilty.*

*Weinig was sentenced to eleven years in prison but lucked out when a Bill Clinton pardon cut his sentence in half. The lawyer also had to forfeit a house and $1.4 million in cash.*

\* \* \* \* \*

### *Headline – <u>How an AT&T Lifer Came to Allegedly Lead Ring Regular Joes. SEC Says Mr. Brumfield Got Tips on Takeover Targets and Passed Them to His Pals.</u>*

*For most of three decades, Charles Brumfield lived in the high life at AT&T Corporation. He started as a sandblaster and rose to one of the most important labor-relations jobs in corporate America. Even as AT&T laid off 100,000 workers, he kept labor peace, lubricating his friendships with Beefeater martinis, gambling and nightly prowls on the town. But something went wrong for Charlie Brumfield. In the late 1980's he began orchestrating what grew into one of the most widespread and long-running insider trading rings of this decade. He gleaned tips on companies targeted by AT&T for takeover and bestowed them like favors, demanding cash kickbacks in return, federal investigators say.*

*It is a tale of betrayal and greed, 1990's style. Mr. Brumfield, 52 years old, betrayed the company that had employed him since high school and put him through college. After he was caught, he betrayed the pals he had tipped. Ultimately, as federal investigators closed in on him, Mr. Brumfield would betray even his own son, Joey. Many at AT&T were shocked when they learned Mr. Brumfield was at the top of this trading pyramid. Why would someone who held one of the most important jobs in American labor chuck it all for a couple of hundred grand? "Charlie? That's what most people around here kept saying when we heard about it, "recalls a senior executive at AT&T. "You've got to be kidding!"*

Sound familiar?

So how does one explain such actions by these people? The answer lies not in stupidity, but rather in their lack of understanding that what they have participated in demonstrating, to those paying attention, is a natural principle of life. While it may be a platitude to say, "junk in, junk out," or for that matter, *"what goes around comes around"*, it is also the truth and the way it actually is!

Nor is this principle limited to the workings of individual lives. In fact, there have been countless examples of people apparently deceived to feel safer committing or participating in lowly actions when they are committed as part of a business or government activity. Presumably they are encouraged by the false sense of security engendered by a "safety in numbers" mentality.

Regardless of the rationale, the Principle applies. On December 25, 1997, the *New York Times* ran the following article:

> ### Headline – <u>30 Firms to Pay $900 Million In Investor Suit. Deal By Brokers Ends Big Price-Fixing Case.</u>
>
> *Thirty brokerage firms, including some of the biggest and most trusted names on Wall Street, agreed yesterday to pay about $900 million to end a civil suit contending they schemed with one another for years to fix prices on the NASDAQ stock market.*
>
> *Lawyers for the plaintiffs in the class action lawsuit, which represented tens of thousands of investors, called it the biggest settlement ever of a price-fixing lawsuit.*

This is not to suggest that this penalty put any of the firms involved out of business. The dollars they paid were the least of their headaches in this matter. The incremental legal expenses involved were most likely substantial, but the cost in terms of the time and attention required to put out this fire flamed by individuals throughout the various organizations is not measurable.

The point is that people within these organizations, went about their lowly activities unaware that they were setting in motion an inevitable chain of responses that would be very costly in their toll on the firms themselves. Those who participated put themselves, the public, and their companies at incalculable risk, not unlike the villains of the 2008 financial crisis that we've lived through, and continue to feel the effects of.

Again, sound familiar? Witness the debacle of corporate integrity revealed by the deeds of senior and rank and file employees of Wells Fargo and Volkswagen.

# IGNORANCE IS NOT BLISS

Consider the following:

- "In one of the biggest criminal cases in municipal finance, a former partner at a major investment banking firm was found guilty of defrauding his clients by failing to disclose a kickback contract with another major firm."

- "The ex-chief of an important charity was sentenced to seven years in prison for looting the coffers of one of the nation's largest charities."

- "In a tale of betrayal and greed, one of America's top labor relations executives was caught leading one of the most widespread and longest running insider trading rings of this decade."

- "After a two year probe, the Senate Ethics Committee found 'substantial cause' to conclude that one of the Senate's most powerful men may have abused his office by sexually harassing over a dozen women over a period of more than 20 years." What???

- "A former treasurer of a large church's governing body was arrested yesterday on charges that he embezzled $800,000 from the church to finance a lavish lifestyle."

- "Ten guards at a county jail were charged with smuggling food, vodka and what they thought was cocaine to prisoners in exchange for bribes and favors."

- "Fourteen police officers were arrested on charges of taking bribes and shaking down drug dealers."

These are all events that actually occurred some years ago. Amazing how they sound so familiar to recent events. Just illustrates how tough it is to bang home the truth about *how life REALLY works.*

Fast forward, and an entire volume could be devoted to the #MeToo Movement alone. To the abuse inflicted on many, over decades, by the likes of Harvey Weinstein, Charlie Rose, Larry Nassar and many others.

Another volume will no doubt be written about the forced resignation of Cardinal Thomas McCarrick, after news of his sexual abuse of children over the course of decades -- and the bombshell, mother of all revelations, of the systemic abuse of multiple thousands of children by more than 300 Catholic priests over a period of more than 70 years. And all this in the State of Pennsylvania alone.

Decades... more than 70 years -- but now the shoe drops — echoes of Emerson...

- "Though no checks to a new evil appear, the checks exist and will appear."
- "Every crime is punished, every virtue rewarded, every wrong redressed."
- "The retribution is inseparable from the thing, but often spread over time."
- "The offense and the punishment grow out of one stem, cause and effect."
- "Seeds and fruit cannot be severed. The affect already blooms in the Cause.

There's no doubt that this massive culture of abuse of many children, over many years, took a masterful cover-up that would be the envy of any criminal enterprise. Or I should say, would have been, up until to the Pennsylvania Grand Jury's announcement of their findings.

But they were smart, those priests. Humans have intelligence. The way they moved those bad people to different parishes, multiple times, kept the recommendations coming, praised their devotion to their flock, all to cloak their evil. Wow, smart!

They were clever, those priests. Humans have the power - the gift of choice! Clever the way they chose to let politicians know what charges they should or should not pursue, if they wanted the Church's political support.

Smart and clever! The combo can keep things going for a long time, depending on the level of skill of the perpetrator. Can't deny those priests had the skill. Just like Harvey Weinstein. Just like Bernie Madoff. Just like Larry Nassar.

It works until it stops working. Why is it that way? How did this set-up come to be? Sorry again, but nobody currently living or who has ever lived, truly knows or knew the answer to that question. But that there are laws that work? Now that is something we actually do know.

# THE LONG REACH OF PRINCIPLE

There is a tendency on the part of many to think that people who are wealthy and powerful are somehow not subject to the same rules of the game, as everyone else. Not so!

In fact, there is a powerful force propelled by nature to correct inequities in human experience, just as it does in the physical world. In human terms of time and evidence, it may be difficult to see this force at work, but rest assured, it is there progressing away nonetheless. Whether caught and punished or not, these individuals lived every moment of every day, knowing not only what they had done, but also that the possibility of their capture at any moment was very real indeed. As Eliot and countless others have proven conclusively, even the highest in station and supposed safety from scrutiny are subject to it.

*And so it goes...*
*Each day another story of woe.*
*Don't They Know???*
*WHAT GOES AROUND...*
*COMES AROUND!*
*Thankfully, however...*
*There is an equally*
*positive aspect*
*to this basic*
*law of life.*
*Take, for example...*

# A Story About Glen

*He is one of the best people I know, and if I had to gather the three or four most honest, reliable and effective people I know, he would be one of them. I first met Glen almost thirty years ago and have worked with him in one capacity or another for more than twenty. During that time I have had the experience of witnessing him come through for others, express good judgement in decision making, maintain poise in the face of daunting pressure to do otherwise, being creative in seeking solutions, and championing countless people in career and personal growth.*

*Part of our work together has involved building a global philanthropy to help children. As great as it is, and as much work as it's taken from both of us, it's only one of many compelling charitable causes that Glen has supported over the years I've known him.*

*Not surprisingly, Glen has trusted friends who would walk through walls for him and do just about anything to pitch in if he ever needed support in any way. He is also one of the most universally liked and respected people I know, and one of the very few I have never heard a negative word spoken about.*

*Topping it all off is Glen's marriage to a lovely lady and their three beautiful children. And this is where I will get off the praise wagon to go to a dark moment I once encountered with Glen, way back.*

*I'm not sure if I'm the only person who knows what I'm about to describe, as he probably expressed the same deep thoughts and feelings to others at the time, but I wouldn't be surprised if I was the only one who remembers. The thing is, one would never describe Glen as a depressive type of person. He was then, like now, virtually always of good cheer, and fun to be around, whether on the golf course, at a bar or in the office. He also seemed to be pretty well settled, living in a house near where he'd grown up in Staten Island, married to a young woman he'd known since high school, and with a promising career under way. So it was jarring when the conversation we were having veered off on this particular day, in the direction it took.*

*We were in the office talking about one of my daughters who had just been in a school play. I was gushing away about her stellar performance as a tree! It had been our usual lively conversation until then, when I became aware that he'd stiffened up and his mood had darkened noticeably. When I asked if he was okay he said,*

*"Yea, I'm never going to have children. Not for me!"*

*It took me aback! "Why would you say that?" I asked. "You're a young guy. You don't have to cross that bridge right now one way or the other, but you'd make a great dad. At least keep the door open."*

*"Nope, ain't gonna happen!"*

*We sat quietly for a while. Then he went on.*

*"Kids are just too damn much trouble. I would never want to go through what my parents went through raising us. That kind of heartache? No thanks."*

*"The time will come you'll change your mind."*

*"Nope, not for me!"*

*I was thinking about what I should say next when one of the guys who worked with us knocked on the door and asked if he could come in. Simultaneously we burst out...*

*"Yea sure come on in. We were just finishing up."*

*And with that, the subject was put to rest, never to be brought up again.*

*Now fast forward about year and a half later. Glen and his wife had divorced, and after all the adjustments and trauma, he had settled in and befriended a single mom with a ten year old son. I started hearing we did this, took the kid there, we did that.*

*"What's happening" I asked one day.*

*"Waddya mean?" He asked in his best Staten Island.*

*"Oh nuthin"*

*"No come on, tell me."*

*"Well, so...ya like this girl and her kid?"*

*"Yea, they're nice, What's not to like?"*

*"Not a thing! I'm just asking."*

*"Oh! Well, yea I guess."*

*"You guess?"*

*"Yea I guess. All right? I guess!"*

*"You guess? All right! You guess! That's good!"*

*"It's good?"*

*"Yea, what's not to be good?"*

*"Nuthin'!"*

*"Yea like I said, it's good."*

*"Ok."*

*"Ok."*

*Not long after that conversation came the invitation to meet for a drink.*

*"There's gonna to be a wedding. Wanna come?"*

*The thing is, everyone comes away from their formative lives with their version of what is true that will effect them for the duration unless something intervenes. No one knows how this set-up came to be, or what the mechanism is for a particular person to either break free or not break free, to change or not change. Some are blessed with whatever it is, some not.*

*You probably think you know where this is going, don't you? Well, for once you may be right! And no, I didn't say a word when he came into my office one day and asked me to grab a sandwich with him.*

*"She's pregnant." He said.*

*"Wow congratulations, that's awesome!*

*"Yea, it' exciting. Really great!*

*"Yea really great!"*

*"Yea"*

The message in "A Story About Glen," is pretty much the same as for all the stories herein and the book as a whole. Glen is a fundamentally good-hearted, generous and well intentioned person. Like every other living being he has had his challenges, troubles and disappointments. But he is also blessed, and its no mystery why to anyone who knows him well.

It's simply because he is such a blessing to each of them!

# LUCK

There is a rumor going around that *luck* is making a come-back as an explanation for the circumstances and conditions of one's life. It certainly can contribute to minimizing the confusion and the guilt we may feel – and be an appealing place to go when everything seems to be going the wrong way, as in, what the hell just happened?

There are certainly cases where I would much prefer to attribute certain things happening to bad luck! In truth though, when push comes to shove and retrospection induced, I can usually find the reason for whatever my challenge might be, right square in the first mirror that I come across.

Still, the subject has been raised! The question of, *what is the role of luck in this life that we live?* Research has been conducted about the many superstitions related to luck, including study of the *lucky* and *unlucky* symbols found in Christian, Chinese, Greek, Navajo and other cultures. Many religions, polytheistic and otherwise have gods and goddesses of luck.

Also, we know from available literature and legend that it has been a topic of much speculation, interest and debate for the duration of our bipedal opposable-thumb existence! So it does cry out for attention here, and I would be remiss in leaving an important gap unaddressed in my effort to explain, *how life really works*, in as comprehensive a manner as possible.

You hear it expressed in many ways:

- *"The only luck I get is bad luck."*
- *"That Johnny just always seems to be down on his luck."*
- *"Man, did that guy luck-out to get that job."*

- *"With my luck I'll be the one person in the show who actually breaks a leg."*

- *"I only lost because she had the luck of the draw."*

- *"Yea we tried, but we just ran out of luck."*

- *"Wow, were we in luck that the place was still open."*

Luck has been described as some force that appears to operate in a person's life to bring in good or bad circumstances, to attract success or failure as the result of chance. It is something that shapes events, opportunities and fortunes – and is beyond a person's control. Belief in luck would seem to hinge on the acceptance that events, even significant ones, can happen by chance, without rhyme or reason, and that they do happen continuously in the human experience. Some consider it to be an actual attribute of a person, ("That lucky devil!") Others believe it can be purchased, or traded for, prayed for or pleaded for. Clearly it can be good or bad.

Personally, I lean more toward the view expressed by the well-known saying: *"The harder I work, the luckier I get!"*

A ten-year study concluded that for the most part, people make their own luck due to the following:

- They are skilled at creating and noticing chance opportunities.

- They make good decisions by listening to their intuitions.

- They create self-fulfilling prophecies by having positive expectations and taking action.

- They exhibit a resilient attitude in the face of difficult challenges, and forge what appears to be good luck.

It is interesting, but also complicating, in that even these observations are far from definitive.

Where I admit to uncertainty about the subject of luck, are the questions of why one was born to those specific parents rather than some others – why they were born in that community to parents who were prosperous, supportive and valued education, rather than into a less advantaged set of circumstances.

It is a mystery that I do think about. I've heard various explanations that actually make some degree of sense, but also require very large leaps of faith, the sign that while possibly well intentioned, the source is best kept in arms-length perspective.

I've also heard people described as *born lucky*. That can be a reference to those circumstances of birth, or to how that person always seems to "land on their feet," when they fall, or "come up smelling like a rose!"

Personally, I do believe that luck is yet another of those topics that can be debated endlessly with passion. It is one that many have and continue to claim they understand and can explain with crystal clarity. But in the end, it is also one of those questions not possible for any human to really, Really, REALLY know the answer to. Its like many others where, just as you think you're getting a glimpse, the curtain closes, the fog descends, and the lights go out!

I simply conclude that Luck, at least good luck, is something I really hope I have at least my fair share of, though if past is prologue to the future, I'll probably have at least some of the other as well. But in either case, I do think I'll know where to look for the answers as to why...

"Oh mirror, mirror on the wall...."

# Surface Mind - Deep Mind

The word *discipline*, not to mention the concept, is probably not one of the most popular in the English language. It is true, however, that the achievement of even the most modest of goals requires some amount of it. Grasping hold of and maintaining control of the steering wheel of one's life is only achieved to the degree that one does exercise discipline in their commitment to remaining alert and paying attention to the road ahead.

It can be likened to an individual's attempt to improve the condition of their abdomen by employing a regimen of sit-ups and other exercises. The key to success in this endeavor is the consistency with which one engages in it rather than the number of repetitions one achieves. Obviously, there is some minimum number required to make an impact, but one is better off keeping the number manageable and doing it consistently, then setting a very high expectation that makes it daunting to stick with.

In short, it is the discipline applied to *staying with the program*, whatever that program may be, that makes the difference. As usual, that means making positive changes in the cause side of the equation to end up with the desired *effect*.

This is crucial to understand, because over the years, the combination of *collective mind* and life's experiences colored by it, register in the deep recesses of an individual mind and gather their own powerful momentum. Together they form the dominant patterns of thoughts, feelings and beliefs that determine the quality and substance of each one's life as it unfolds.

A positive change to those patterns will inevitably lead to like changes in the resulting quality and substance of that life. Affecting that change, once the patterns are established and embedded is each individual's most imperative challenge.

In this human condition we all find ourselves in, it is helpful to understand that while each individual has a mind which is unique to themselves, that mind operates in two completely distinct ways. These have been referred to as Conscious/Subconscious, Objective/Subjective, and Surface/Depths. The latter will suffice for this discussion.

Think of mind as the ocean. It has both a surface and its unseen depths. The surface may rage with the waves of storms and disturbances. On it may float ships or seaweed, people or foam. Way below the surface, however, one would hardly know what was going on up there at the surface. In fact, only the most persistent and tenacious of activities above make their presence known in the great depths below. Of course the words, *surface* and *depths* are merely descriptive terms. While they connote different aspects of the sea, the ocean is after all, one mass of water, one indivisible whole.

In similar fashion, the human mind has two separate activities going on within it, even though it is one entity. Take for example, learning to play a musical instrument such as a guitar or piano. *Surface mind* directs the playing of each note until finally, after sufficient practice and repetitions, the understanding necessary passes into *deeper mind*, and it becomes automatic.

Surface Mind is, therefore, the conscious, directing aspect of mind. It chooses and selects, considers choices and then decides. All choices are made in this surface aspect of mind and then pass beyond, into the deeper mind where they are recorded for future reference.

Deeper Mind, on the other hand, is where one's life is molded and shaped. It is the factory which takes the raw materials provided by surface mind's choices and the influence of collective mind, and turns them into the quality and substance of life's experiences. It doesn't consider whether those raw materials are good or bad, positive or negative, healthy or unhealthy. It just takes what it is given and translates it into that one's outer condition of life.

The deeper mind does not choose what it accepts. It is simply compelled to take what it is given and work from the patterns provided. Whatever messages come through most consistently and most powerfully become the forces that either continue the status quo or act as positive or negative agents of change. The way to make sure that it acts as an agent of change in the positive sense, is to purposefully and consistently provide one's deeper mind with a higher quality of input from surface mind choices. Even the powerful influences of collective mind can be overcome by consistent persistence.

While it is clearly not easy for someone to change their habitual ways of thinking and reacting, nevertheless it can be done. Motivation to do so can be derived from grasping the fact that it is the blended level of the thought contained in one's deeper mind that creates their outer circumstances. This includes who a person currently is and what prospects they have for the future. Before appearing in one's outer world, circumstances and conditions are first established in deeper mind, based on the influences of collective mind and surface mind.

*This is a process that can be taken charge of at any time.*

Thought is an ongoing activity which is never still. Whether you like it or not, you are always providing input of some nature to deeper mind. So, how do you make sure that the nature of the input in question is what you intend or desire?

It is certain that negative thoughts, once established in deeper mind, will in due time create something in outer life experience that corresponds to them. The same can be said for positive, forward-thinking productive and positive thoughts. They are never wasted and always eventually find their way to the surface of one's experience.

It may not be apparent how that good will show up, but every kindness, every positive thought, every action of goodness will inevitably yield some measure of happiness, prosperity, joy, health or love. That is the way it works.

There is nothing either fair or unfair about this. It is simply, *how it is.* The encouraging thing to know is that at any moment, an individual can wrest control, purposefully direct positive surface mind inputs, and begin to shift the deeper mind's patterns to produce life experiences in line with one's desires.

# Thoughts To Live By

What follows does not purport to be *the way* to enlightenment, or perfection, or even to self-improvement. It is, however, one way that has helped me and many others, and I hope will prove to be a helpful suggestion for you as well. The short musings that follow have been described as *helpful meditations*. I call them *focus interventions*, and *Thoughts To Live By*, and I do believe that adhering to the guidelines that follow will be a helpful and easily digestible addition to any individuals life, regardless of their particular starting point.

But first a word about *ways*, and *paths*, and the like. Throughout the ages there have been numerous distinguished philosophical and spiritual thinkers and teachers who have inspired countless millions with their words and ideas. The common threads which are found time after time in their messages are:

A. A person's outer life is a reflection of their inner self.

B. The place to turn for the answer to whatever is needed, is within.

*The question is, how does one actually do that – turn within?*

There are innumerable well-established processes to achieve it, including many schools of meditation and yoga. They generally involve various levels of commitment to daily or at least several times a week practice, and the requirement of committing certain amounts of time on a consistent basis. They may also require practitioners to travel to and from a gathering place or studio.

If you are reading this and saying, "Yup, that's me. All set! Got that part down and really like doing my yoga or meditation practices. I easily get through to the quiet place and the answers jump right out at me," that is great! No need to change anything you're doing. Just perhaps to add a new arrow to the quiver for use when needed.

For all the rest of you who don't have previously established practices, if you are like me and can rarely find the time, the place, or the patience to meditate, then good news! For you, the following may make a significant contribution!

I think of it as *how to calm the raging beast*, and find it a particularly helpful tool for situations when I am gripped by some strong and unproductive feeling that I would rather not have. Feelings like fear, anger and resentment can change your mood for the worse and take you out of the good state of mind you were in before they struck. They debilitate your energy, and have no useful purpose.

*But when you're stuck in them, how can you escape to get beyond?*

*The answer presented here is to wrest your attention away from whatever thoughts and feelings have you in their grip, and focus instead on short statements like the ones that follow. You can read one through once or many times. You can refer to it several times over the course of the day, whatever it takes to "crush the beast."*

The premise behind this activity is neither religious, nor philosophical, nor spiritual. It is purely mechanical. It is simply that you can't possibly have your attention on two things at the same time. By exercising the discipline to focus on one of the pages that follow or others like them, you are taking control and giving yourself "the way forward!"

It is no different from the *mantras* taught over the ages as a pathway into meditation, except that in this case, meditation is not the goal. Here you simply, want to purposely change the trajectory of your thoughts from a negative and self-destructive path to at least a neutral, and hopefully a positive one. That alone will have an impact on the *cause* side of your *cause/effect* equation.

The following includes a few contributions to this cause. There are enough for each day of a month. They can be repeated, used in all or parts, or as inspiration to create your own. It is well established that dwelling on even one word that upholds higher values, can produce profound physiological and psychological changes, lower the heart beat and blood pressure, calm the nerves and quiet the mind.

I personally like to read short statements like the ones that follow. There are days when I may refer to it several times. But if a single word works for you, by all means use it. Examples would be – peace, light, calm.

I can attest to having saved myself a great deal of misery by developing the mental muscle to force my attention to make the move described above. It is the mechanism by which my *Surface Mind* changes the message being sent to my *Deeper Mind* and gives me a fighting chance to improve the circumstances and conditions of my life. It is what I wish for you, and moreover, it is actually ... *How Life REALLY Works!* :)

# *I Am Constantly Inspired*

- I know that I have within me the source of every answer I will ever need, and I open myself to that source right now. I clear away any thought or idea of limitation or dependency on any person, place or thing outside of myself. I am aware only of the flow of intelligence through me.

- The direction I require in this situation, in this moment, is clearly conveyed by the inner voice that speaks to me when I am prepared to listen. I resolve now to be prepared at all times and as a result, I listen intuitively, I hear only the truth, and I know only that which is good and my experience of life is wonderful in every way.

- I am renewed constantly by the inspiration I receive by staying open and connected to my own personal source within. Right ideas continuously flow to me accompanied by the energy to make them happen for the greater good of myself and all those who are important to me. Through my clarity, I know what I am doing and I do it now!

# I Am a Work of Art

- I am truly an unbelievable creature of the universe, a veritable work of art. I am a totally unique and individual expression of life. After all, who else has the particular talents and abilities, friendships and family members, education and training, feelings and sensitivities as I do? Really, there is nobody and that is an idea that I treasure.

- Yes, I am a work of art, but I have yet to fully live up to all of my potential. There is so much more within me to be expressed, more than even I am aware is possible, in every area of my life. I do, however, have all that I need, right now, to express more fully all the talents and abilities that life has given me. I resolve to do so now.

- I make the commitment in this very moment to spend my time engaged in activities that fully support development as the person I choose to be. I put my energy squarely behind this effort and purposefully disengage from whatever does not contribute, regardless of how it may have gripped me in the past. I declare myself free to chart my own course. What's more, I am the only one who can. What a great idea that is!

# I Am Directed and Clear

- I recognize that I have the power of choice today, that determines the quality of my life's experience tomorrow. Therefore, I wisely consider everything that I think, say and do. I am the selector in my life. I declare myself to be free to make those selections that contribute to my greatest good.

- I make sure that I am always aware of what is going on that affects my life. I stay awake, alert and on the ball. I exercise my life-given intelligence to stay organized and on top of everything related to my life's interests. If something needs to be done, I do it. If an attitude adjustment is required, I look in the mirror and get it done.

- I progress steadily toward my well-defined goals, minimizing wasted time and energy and maximizing my life-given talents and abilities. I have no intention of realizing at some later date that I have wasted my life on meaningless thoughts and activities. Everything that I do has a purpose and the result is great!

# *My Life Is Creation*

- My life is the unfolding of a rich flow of ideas passing through my mind. I know and accept that I can create in my experience anything that my mind can conceive, and this conviction creates only new, fresh and vital experiences every day.

- They literally pour into my life creating a wonderful pattern of great and dynamic relationships, interesting and prosperous work experiences and satisfying opportunities for creative self-expression. Life is fulfilled by operating through me. I willingly and happily enjoy the ride. I accept and act upon the great ideas that are revealed to me.

- Creation happens in my life through me, by means of the ideas that I choose to express and the intelligence, energy and appreciation I apply to them. I choose those thoughts with life centered wisdom. I act on them with the full force and power of self-directed focus. They unfold in perfection.

# *In Harmony with Right Action*

- I know that I can experience a wonderful, loving and prosperous life by remaining ever in harmony with the universal law of right action, and I do. Everything I do, say and think combine in harmonious acceptance of only the best in my life, and nothing can sway me from the quiet strength of this conviction. I move forward with calm determination to my ever-increasing satisfaction and fulfillment.

- Detractors may abound, but here within the peace of my inner self, I have all the support I need. There is a deep conviction within me that nothing can hold me back but my own choices, so I make sure through wise consideration that they are the right ones.

- I find the right path for me and follow it with all the power, strength and conviction of my being, to my rightful and natural destination. If I am diverted from my chosen path momentarily, I recognize it, then without fuss or self-criticism, get back on. Right action accompanies my every step because right thinking paves my way. This is my truth right now!

# I Handle My Responsibilities

- I am a poised and confident individual with a quiet sense of authority over my life and its responsibilities. I accept them gladly. I recognize them as gifts to assist the process of my personal development, and I handle them easily and effectively.

- There is a positive and powerful life energy that surges through my entire being and propels me through all my activities. I get everything done that is needed to achieve and fulfill my goals and responsibilities, efficiently and successfully, and through it all, I remain happy, positive and focused.

- I have a sense of inner peace, knowing that there is nothing that can come my way that I can't handle with ease. I have the wisdom of the world at my disposal and the intelligence to use it. I am blessed with a quiet sense of myself that welcomes every challenge that appears. I feel good, I do good and I am good.

# I Trust My Judgement

- I take the responsibility of decision-making very seriously, especially when my decisions impact the lives of others, which is usually the case. My decisions are born of wisdom and acted upon with the strength of knowing that I am guided by life's source of intelligence in all that I do.

- I trust my judgement implicitly and know that order governs my life and the lives of all those I care about. I have no concern or fear as I go about the business of backing up that judgement with action. I put the pedal to the metal, knowing without question that the direction I am moving in is correct.

- I know that when I combine responsibility, good judgement and positive energy, there is no way that I can fall off the track and not achieve the desired results or better. Any surprises that come my way have to be positive ones. I welcome them as perfectly normal and natural results of life working as it should.

# *I See Clearly*

- My thinking is clear as I go through life today. I am completely tuned to the intelligence and source within that connects me with all of life. There is no confusion as situations and challenges present themselves, because I see clearly, reason logically and reach sensible and correct conclusions.

- I know that the power which supports and directs all that I do comes from within. I release any notion that places that power outside of myself and I get attuned and unify with it. There is nothing I cannot do through the inner power that strengthens and uplifts me.

- I recognized the perfect order and symmetry of the universe in nature and in my life and dedicate myself to expressing only that which creates beauty, joy, health, harmony and prosperity. I see the larger picture, the whole picture. I know what to do and I do it now! Life is great and I love living it.

# I Have a Wonderful Life

- I have a wonderful life, full of beauty, love, happiness, harmony and prosperity. Everything I do is geared toward completely constructive and productive activities. I give absolutely zero time and energy to petty feelings that tear away at my focus and strength and produce nothing positive in my life. I gladly turn away from them and they slip away now.

- I concentrate my focus and vision on what I wish to experience. I have high expectations for myself and am careful that I do not waste my time and energy on feelings and activities which do not contribute toward the realization of those expectations. I let go of anything and everything that does not measure up.

- I identify myself with activities that produce good for myself and others. I see clearly what to do and I follow through with vitality and energy now. Everything I do is with the expectation of success because I know I am supported by all of life's positive forces and guided by life's deepest intelligence. I am a good, complete and whole person and the people and triumphs I experience in my life reflect it.

# *It Is Great to Be Alive*

- It is great to be alive and I live my life as a personification of all that is great about it. I am one with goodness, happiness, joyfulness, cheerfulness, friendliness, truthfulness, generosity and all that is positive and I wish the same for every person I meet.

- Great things are constantly showing up in my life. My work produces personal recognition and ever-increasing income, my investments produce terrific returns, my relationships with family, friends and colleagues constantly bring me happiness. I am totally appreciative of all my good and am diligent to assure that my thoughts, feelings, words and actions are all conducive to staying in that flow.

- Whatever limitations or blocks to my good may have been present in the past are no longer part of my being and no longer have any power or control over my attitudes or my life. Only goodness, only love, only happiness, only appreciation reside here, and that's the way I like it!

# *Freedom Is Mine*

- I claim my freedom now. I know deep down within me, with all the intelligence that I possess, that I am free. There is nothing that can prevent me from experiencing the best that life has to offer. I am free from fear, free from envy, free from doubt and free from the feeling that I lack anything at all.

- I am deeply thankful for all the good that I possess and all the wondrous good that flows steadily into my life. I am profoundly grateful for my freedom to pursue my hopes and dreams and the inspiration, drive and dogged stick-to-it-tiveness, to make them a reality.

- I am inspired by the knowingness that I possess life's greatest gift, the precious understanding that I am truly free to live fully, to love passionately, to express my potential powerfully, to achieve peace of mind, joy, love and prosperity. Life is truly rich and I am the most willing recipient of all its treasures.

## On the Brink

- There is a plan for my life. It is to live it the best I can and to express myself in the highest possible way. I know that it is entirely up to me and nobody else to do this. I am responsible for my life and I have every intention of seeing that it is a great success.

- I can do with my life entirely what I please. My choice is to live it with meaning and purpose. I put positive energy behind my ideas and take action when I recognize an opportunity to affect someone or something in a positive manner.

- I am very grateful for the many wonderful people and experiences I have enjoyed so far in life and look forward with anticipation to what's on the way. I know that I'm on the brink of something wonderful and I get ready for it by putting everything I have into the business of living my life. I give my all to everything that I do and life returns only the best to me in kind.

# I Attract Only Good

- There are no limits on the quantity of good or the quality of life that I experience. There is nothing I cannot do, nowhere I cannot go and nothing I cannot be, if I can conceive of it, believe in it and am willing to grow into the potential that I know exists to make it so.

- I declare my connection with that which is greater than I. It supports me completely. I know and accept this truth and have total confidence in myself. I act out of courage and have no fear. Why should I? I cooperate with the wonder of life and through that wonder only good things express themselves in my life.

- Wisdom and understanding guide me every step of the way and I have faith that only good comes to me, around me and through me. Everyone who has contact with me is positively affected by the experience as I reflect life's intelligence expressing its best as me.

# I Live from the Highest Vantage Point

- I commit to live my life today from the highest vantage point. The dress rehearsal is over and the curtain has gone up. This is the real thing and I am ready for it. Whatever may have conspired to hold me back from being my best no longer has any hold on me. There is no anchor to my progress. There is only progress.

- There is absolutely no place is my life, attitudes or behavior for the trivial or second rate from me. The only reviews I want are raves. My life is a living statement of good intentions, and they are clearly rewarded by the prodigious quantities of good that flow to me. I am the chooser in my particular world and I choose well.

- I contemplate all aspects of life from the highest point of view. I am a good person, striving to be better. My health, wealth, personal relationships and enjoyment of life all reflect it. In fact, my life is a great example of how good things can be. This is the way I choose to approach living, and I do so consistently and enthusiastically.

# *I Am Guided to Right Action*

- I have the anticipation and the expectation that all upcoming events will be great for me and for everyone else involved. I know that everyone's best interests, mine included, will be served and have complete faith that it is so.

- I approach my world with courage and certainty that I am guided to right actions. There is no reason for it to be any other way. I have great tools for handling life and I appreciate them immensely. The wisdom and understanding of life are mine to use and I use them well to express the best of me.

- Everything I do today exemplifies life's highest ideals. There is nothing that stands in my way except my own misuse of the life force within me, and I purposefully ensure that is not the case. I know that I am the architect of my own life's experience and I choose the elements with which I construct it with care. I choose only the best and the results reflect it.

# *I Create the Best Possible me*

- I am a whole person, completely in touch with the life force flowing through me. All my various elements work together to create the best possible expression of life in human form ... me! Mind and body blend in perfect harmony within me!

- I have one purpose in life and that is to associate myself only with the truth, the good, the noble. The result is a person greater than the sum total of all my parts. Everything I need to fulfill my life falls easily in place and all resistance to my good just falls away. The life force operating through the harmonious being that I am, generates an awesome display of effective living.

- I can do all things. I work easily and well, because there is no blockage within me. All the channels are open and I keep them that way with right thinking and right actions. I live to express the highest and best of life and I make sure that everything I think, say and do is coordinated with that purpose.

# *I Put Legs on My Ideas*

- One of the great gifts bestowed upon human beings is freedom of choice, and I use mine to achieve the best I am capable of. I do what needs to be done to move forward in life effectively. No grass grows under these feet. I have a clear idea of what I want to achieve and nothing stands in the way of its full and complete expression.

- It is clear that I am the only one capable of doing what is needed to achieve my goals, so I put legs on my ideas and get moving on them now. When procrastination takes me in its grasp, I simply relax, remember who and what I am and get back on track. I love the feel of life's force moving through me to achieve my goal. I do what is needed and go where I must, to get on with the business of living right now.

- I am happy, and even eager, to claim all the good that life has for me. Obstacles are no match for the power of my ideas, infused with life's energy, working through me at my direction. What can oppose such a force? Nothing really. Quite the opposite. Everything supports it. What a great notion.

# *I Get My Life in Order*

- I look around at the universe that surrounds me and see order and balance. All of nature seems to have a rhyme and reason. I resolve to get my life in order now. I go about living my life easily and effectively. I maintain my composure no matter how tempestuous external conditions may be. Within me is a pattern of harmony and order that will prevail.

- My mind remains quiet and free from fear and I am always able to think clearly no matter how confusing things may seem to be. I am a whole and perfectly balanced person. It shows in how I handle both success and adversity. Success points out that I am heading in the right direction. I make note and keep going. Failure, merely points out that it is my attitude that requires adjustment rather than some other person or condition needing to change. This frees me to make changes to something that I can control, me!

- I see the beauty and symmetry of the universe in my own life. Storms may rage but at my core is the calm found in the deepest part of the sea, the perfect order of the seasons, and the wondrous inspiration of the stars. The intelligence of life guides me in all I do, say and think, with wisdom and understanding. My life is in perfect balance at all times.

# I Choose Happiness

- Personally, I prefer being a happy person to being a miserable one, and I declare now, my commitment to clear out all the negative ideas, fears, resentments, anger and the like, which block that happiness I desire. I believe that life is meant to be lived happily. I am supposed to be happy. I am happy.

- It is incorrect thinking and actions that cause lack of happiness. I determine that they no longer lay any claim on me. I don't know where they came from or what caused them, but I'm not wasting any more of my life and energy on them. They are history. What my mind dwells on is entirely my choice. I exercise that choice to dwell on what is right about the world and my life.

- I am now clear in mind and heart. I see only the good and only the good comes back to me. As the man said, I contemplate life from the highest point of view and, as a result, the highest good of life is what I experience. I trust everyone in my world to respond to me with goodness and am not surprised when I am trusted in kind. My goal is to be completely happy in life. To achieve it, I am willing to do whatever is needed. I allow nothing to block its expression in my life.

# I Cooperate for the Greatest Good

- The idea of cooperation is a cornerstone of my philosophy of life. My actions and attitudes reflect it. Basically, I cooperate with life and life cooperates with me. I cooperate with life by joining "the team". My concern is to facilitate the greatest good for the greatest number of people. I know that by taking that approach, my own personal good is assured as well, so I hold nothing back.

- My real, secret goal is to contribute to making this world a better place to live, for this and future generations. To do this, I cooperate fully with life. I let go of personal fears, concern, anger, envy, etc. and remember that I am on Life's Team. I know that those negatives only block my good anyway and I easily let them go. The result is that my own life's experience is dramatically enhanced.

- My interest is only in the greater good. I cooperate with people to achieve it. Inner wisdom, free from the restraints of negativity, shows me the way and I follow, willingly and enthusiastically. The alternative is to wallow in misery, bringing nothing but grief to myself and others. That is not an acceptable choice for me and I reject it out of hand. I see it as the road to my own demise and I avoid it by turning my attention to only that which supports my good. How great to know that I have the power to make that choice. Wow, life is great!

# I Appreciate All My Good

- I approach my world today with complete confidence in my ability to handle every challenge that presents itself and a sense of really enjoying the process of life that I am participating in. Everyone who meets me is left with a positive impression because of how nicely and effortlessly I seem to deal with life, and they are correct. I am right smack in the flow of success and prosperity, and I am having the time of my life.

- Whatever comes up to greet me today is well within my ability to handle easily. Whatever may have held me back or caused fear in the past, no longer has any power over me. Why should it? Today, I am the me of now, not the me of yesterday. I know more now than I did then. Most importantly, I know that I am in charge of such things. I move onward and upward to greater, more rewarding success in all areas of my life and I enjoy myself thoroughly as I do.

- I see everyone I meet as a positive contributor to my experience and growth and gladly treat them accordingly. My attitude toward this matter is determined not by their approach to me, but by what I purposefully choose my attitude to be. Having said that, I fully expect a wonderful attitude from everyone I meet. There is no reason or need for it to be any other way. This makes my life all the more wonderful and it is!

# *I Align Myself with Good*

- I am aware of my every thought and feeling and I resolve now to use them intelligently to form only patterns of success, harmony, health and happiness. My intention is to align myself only with the good, the true, and the perfect, and I do that now!

- I know the kind of person I want to be. All my actions are in line with producing a life that is noble and good. I accept that I am the living embodiment of the beliefs and ideas that I hold in mind, so I am careful to indulge in only those thoughts by which I wish to be known.

- I am guided and protected by an intelligence and wisdom which inspires me with enthusiasm. Everything that I do, say and think expresses this intelligence, as I move easily and confidently through this great experience of life!

# I Am Free

- Today I cease all concerns and worry about myself and everyone else. I totally let go and stop trying to make things happen. At this moment, I declare myself free to move away from outer appearances, and petty concerns, and toward the quiet of that place where my true self connects with universal good.

- I relax and let go, knowing there is nothing I must do to receive the good that is now flowing into my life. I simply accept and enjoy the feeling, as health, prosperity, friendship and happiness envelope me. I am mentally, emotionally and physically ready and willing to allow all of life's good to come my way.

- There may have been a time when negative mental attitudes commanded my attention and debilitated the quality of my life. Knowing what I know now that is no longer the case. It seems so silly that it could have been. In any event, they are long gone. I expect only good, and that is exactly what I get.

# I Take the High Road

- I make the conscious choice today to take the high road in every situation I face. If I have the opportunity to be critical, I'm not. If anger, resentment, fear or envy threaten to dominate my attention, I grasp control of my thinking and don't allow it.

- I maintain my composure in the face of all pressure to do otherwise, secure in the understanding that my best interest is served in doing so. If others wish to descend to the low road of behavior, I simply make the observation and move on. My choices are determined by what I wish to experience and achieve and I refuse to turn over that control to anyone else.

- I simply do the best I can in every situation I encounter. I trust in my own judgment and know that I am in my rightful place and time, moving in the right direction. The result is that everything falls easily into place for everyone's greatest good.

# I Am a Credit to the Race

- I declare myself to be a credit to the human race and everything that I do, say and think backs that conviction up. I am in the right place in life for me at this time and I purposefully fill that place with positive and powerful authority.

- I am a tremendously powerful force in my world and I use this power with wisdom to achieve the best for myself and everyone around me. I do this by aligning myself with high ideals, and infusing myself with positive energy.

- I have no doubt or fear. I am confident, secure and convinced that nothing is too good to be true and nothing is too wonderful to happen in my life. All the forces align to support me in all that I desire to achieve and only good results. This is my truth. I accept it with grateful exuberance.

# I Take Control

- My intention is to be my best and do my best each and every moment. I have the highest of intentions in everything I do and my actions reflect it. My motives are to be a stronger and more effective person and I now take control of my thoughts and feelings, words and actions.

- I purposely let go of any personal characteristics that are not in keeping with the kind of person I declare myself to be and the life I choose to live. Feelings, thought and actions which are not worthy of my time and energy are now eliminated.

- When my attention is taken by negative, habitual ideas, I break their grip by turning to different and better ideas. I am proud of how I go about the business of living this life. I take control of what I think, say and do, and the results reflect it as happiness floods my existence.

# *I Recognize the Good*

- I take time today to recognize the presence of good in all places, in all things and in all people. I strive to recognize the essential core of good at the center of every person I meet. I look out upon my world and see the positives that are present there.

- I am aware of the unmistakable presence of a universal power for good in all areas of my life. Every leaf and blade of grass expresses the perfection that is present in the world and in my life. That perfection has always been there, awaiting only my recognition and claim of it. I do so now, committing myself to the changes in attitude, actions and life, needed to receive and retain it. I declare this as my truth and accept it now.

- The result is a tremendous flow of good into my world. The doors open wide and only the best comes through. I maintain vigilance over all that I do in order to keep it that way. It is easy for me to do this because I now know it is the only way for me to have the quality of life that I desire and deserve.

# I Expect to Be Happy

- I expect today to be happy and productive, free from difficulty or conflict. I expect the best in every situation. It is not necessary for me to know exactly how events will unfold because I know it will turn out to be positive for me and for everyone involved.

- I am not limited by anyone or anything today. Others are welcome to their opinions. I know the truth about myself, and the truth is that I am in complete harmony with my world today.

- Nothing can deter me from this powerful, inner conviction. I connect deeply with my true self and know that only the best that life has to offer is heading my way. When it arrives I accept it as the natural result of who I am and how I live and know without a doubt that more is coming.

# *Dedicated to Full Potential*

- I dedicate myself to living up to my full potential in all areas of my life and in all that I do. I make sure that each and every one of my thoughts, words and actions are in alignment with that idea because I know there is a law of cause and effect operating in my life which produces absolute justice.

- Rather than complaining and blaming everyone and everything but myself for my challenges and struggles, I merely get myself in hand, knowing that that when I am doing the right thing internally, my life reflects it externally. I love this idea and embrace it fully as it puts me firmly in charge of my own life.

- I apply myself to awareness of what I am doing and the effect of it on my world of experience. My thoughts, words and actions blend into the creative substance that gives shape to a wonderful life. Health, happiness, love and prosperity are all mine in ever-increasing quantities.

# I Am Confident in Myself

- I express appreciation in everything I think, feel, say and do. I am deeply grateful for my life and the chance to live it. I experience life as a thrill, and energy literally surges through me as I live it accordingly. I even appreciate my mistakes and errors of judgment for what I learn from them.

- I forgive myself for my shortcomings quickly and easily and I am lifted to new heights of awareness and realization. I appreciate the real self within me. The self that is connected to the intelligence of life, the self that inspires me with truth and understanding.

- I see only the best in others and I appreciate it. I accept that everyone is doing the best they can given their particular level of understanding and I give them the space to be who they are, free of my judgment. I appreciate the world in which I live, the power I have through my choices to change it and the responsibility I have for the quality of my own life.

# More About the Title

A certain grandmother I referenced earlier would respond to life's situations with expressions like:

*"Well Dear, you made your bed, now you can lie in it."*

Another of her favorites was:

*"Ok my Darling, now you can just go and stew in your own juice!"*

Every culture has their own version of these common sense-inspired homilies. They testify that the circumstances one finds oneself in are the result of one's own doing. We may blame everyone and everything else around us, but as Granny so eloquently quipped:

*"Hey Kiddo, nobody made or didn't make the bed, and nobody picked the ingredients of the soup, but you!"*

Now, like many before and after her, Granny had a lot easier time seeing and pointing out the folly of my ways than her own. In fact, in my life, I've provided the perfect opportunity for many people in a wide variety of circumstances to observe my ill-advised choices in life, and have witnessed Granny's affliction in many of them. However, the worst offender I've ever met, greets me daily in the mirror.

We all know that the people around us on some level, are causing their own misery, and may even witness some of them repeat the same destructive actions over and over. It's always seeing that in ourselves which is the trick.

I relayed earlier where and when I first heard the title of this book used to explain the reason for someone's comeuppance, but I've heard it many times since. It is usually spoken by someone in a most reverent and knowing manner.

"Oh well," I can hear them say, *what goes around comes around,* as every-one invariably shakes their head in agreement.

It's as though that says it all. Like some sage wisdom that the speaker learned someplace, but isn't sure where. The fall from grace, was shock-ing at first, but less so when we find out what led up to it. We all intui-tively understand this.

After all, *what goes around... does actually... come around.* We just don't know when!

# Epilogue

What goes on in one's life is the result of the influence of collective mind combined with what one thinks, says and does. To the degree that the individual takes purposeful control of their thoughts, words and actions, they can elevate themselves and their experience of life above the influence and statistical realities of their circumstances and environments.

That is the quest I challenge you with, along with the question:

*What sort of garden of life are you cultivating?*

Understanding and working with the *law of cause and effect* is clearly not a *nice to have* matter, but a *need to have* one. That is so because life doesn't just happen to us by chance. It happens for a reason, and the reason is us!

Now you know! So, good luck in your quest and please.... *plant good seeds!*